U.S. Air Force Historical Study No. 114
(Formerly Army Air Forces Reference History No. 14)
(Short Title – AAFRH-14)

THE
TWELFTH AIR FORCE
IN THE
NORTH AFRICAN WINTER CAMPAIGN
11 NOVEMBER 1942 TO THE REORGANIZATION
OF 18 FEBRUARY 1943

PREPARED BY
AAF HISTORICAL OFFICE
HEADQUARTERS, ARMY AIR FORCES

REFERENCE HISTORY

THE TWELFTH AIR FORCE

IN THE NORTH AFRICAN WINTER CAMPAIGN

11 November 1942 to the Reorganization
of 18 February 1943

(Short Title: AAFRH-14)

The original of this monograph and the documents from which it was written are in the USAF Historical Division, Archives Branch, Bldg. 914, Maxwell Air Force Base, Alabama.

Prepared by
AAF Historical Office
January 1946

FOREWORD

This study, prepared by T/Sgt. Thomas J. Mayock of the Combat Operational History Division, AAF Historical Office, recounts the career of the Twelfth Air Force from the time it became established in newly pacified French North Africa until it was absorbed in the Northwest African Air Forces. A previous study, Air Phase of the North African Invasion, November 1942, has treated the origin of the Twelfth, its pre-invasion development, and the part it played in the North African landings. To give the present work unity and to serve the reader's convenience Air Phase of the North African Invasion has been drawn upon for various background materials appearing in Chapters I and II. Like other studies prepared by the Historical Office, this study is subject to revision as additional information becomes available.

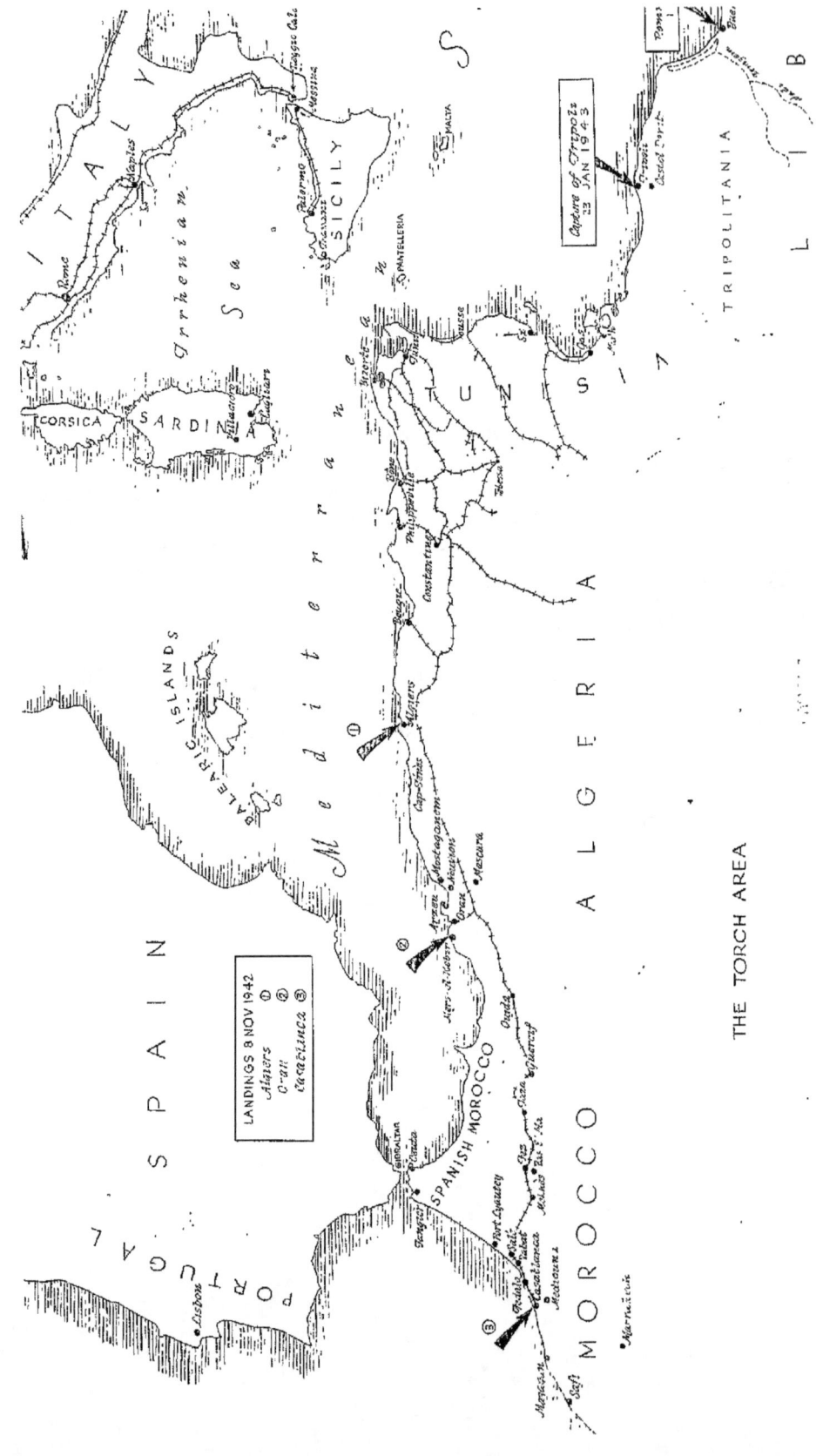

THE TORCH AREA

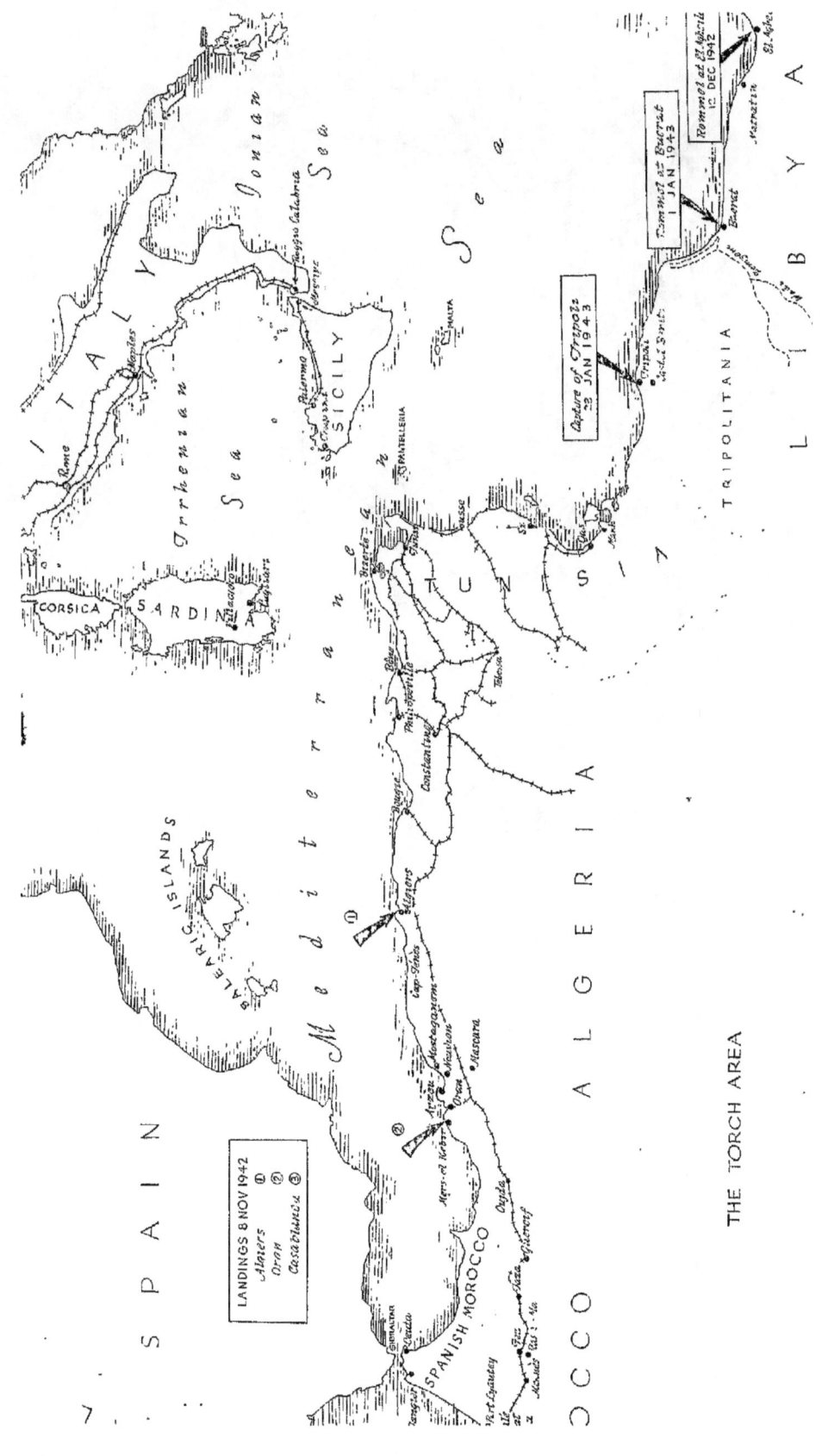

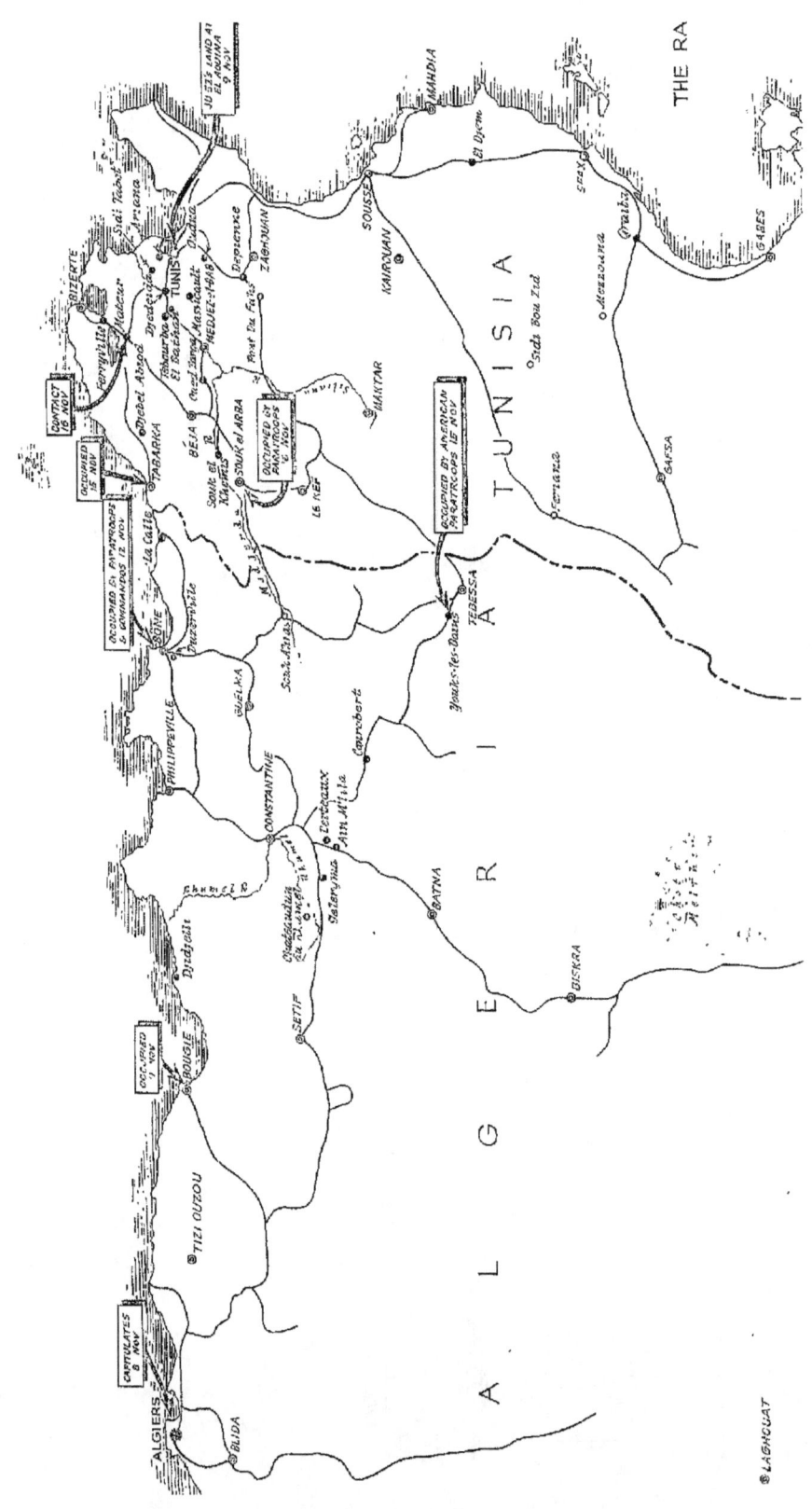

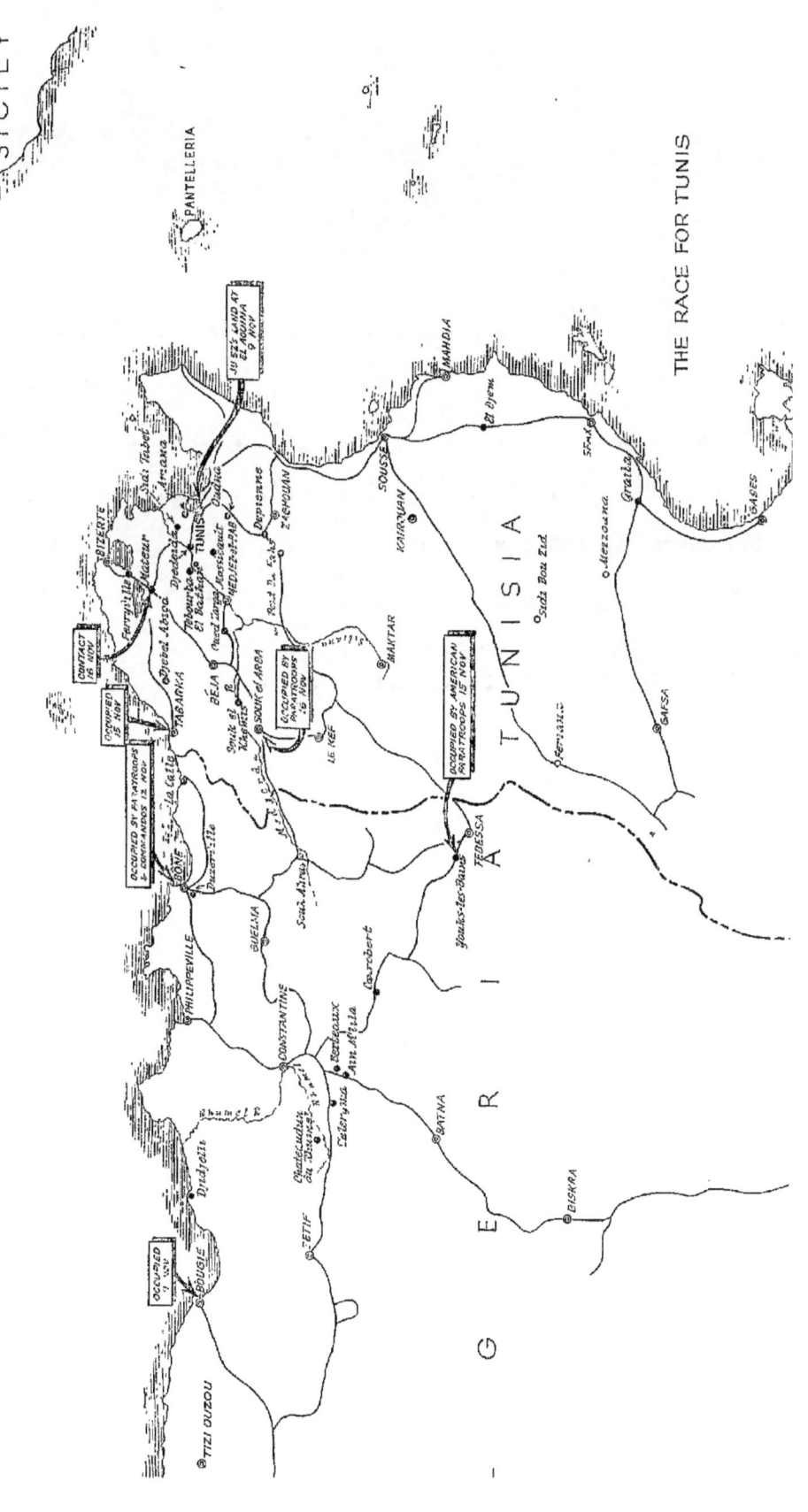

CHARTS

The TORCH Area . . . . Frontispiece

                                                                                                     Following

The Race for Tunis 11

The Battle Area 43

Robaa and Ousseltia Actions 117

Area of II Corps Operations, 31 Jan.-23 Feb. 1943 . . . 164

Organization of Northwest African Air Forces
   and Related Commands, 18 Feb. 1943 180

CONTENTS

I INTRODUCTION 1

II THE RACE FOR TUNIS 7
    Prelude to Tunisia 7
    The Contribution of the C-47's 10
    The Twelfth Moves Eastward 15
    The Drive for Tunis 22
    Stalemate 28
    The German Counterblow 36

III IMPASSE AND REORGANIZATION 42
    The Anatomy of the Repulse 42
    New Air Bases 45
    Bomber Reinforcements 51
    The Assault on the Ports 55
    The Mediums 63
    XII Fighter Command 68
    Internal Reorganization 80

IV THE DEVELOPMENT OF COMMAND AND STRATEGY 88
    The Theater Air Force 88
    The Genesis of the Northwest African Air Forces 97

V AIR-GROUND COOPERATION IN CENTRAL TUNISIA 109
    Operation SATIN 109
    The Allied Air Support Command 114
    Prelude to Kasserine 122

VI XII BOMBER COMMAND--JANUARY AND FEBRUARY 133
    The Logistic Marathon 133
    Minimum-Altitude Attacks against Shipping 136
    The Bomber Offensive 143
    Attrition and the Air War 153
    Performance of the Mediums 159

VII THE TURN OF THE TIDE 163
    The Axis Break-Through 163
    The Crisis before Thala 169
    The Northwest African Air Forces 177
    The Significance of NAAF 182

GLOSSARY 189
NOTES 190
BIBLIOGRAPHICAL NOTE 209
INDEX 210

The Twelfth Air Force in the North African Winter Campaign:
11 November 1942 to the Reorganization of 18 February 1943

Chapter I
INTRODUCTION

Before proceeding to the story of the Twelfth Air Force during its first four months in Africa, it is advisable to review the plans laid in London and Washington for the employment of the Twelfth in the theater. It is particularly advisable in that, in good part, the logic of events determined that these plans were not to be carried out--and only in the realization of the shift in plans and strategy after the landings on 8 November can Twelfth Air Force, or for that matter theater, history be set down. This introduction, in a summary way, recounts therefore the events attending the adoption of the TORCH plan and the conflicting strategies which gave the plan a certain ambivalence. The origins and functions of the Twelfth Air Force and XII Air Support Command are likewise treated in brief.[1]

In mid-April 1942, America and Great Britain had apparently agreed on a firm strategy for the extinction of the European Axis: cross-Channel invasion following a preparatory day-and-night air offensive. Target date for ROUND-UP, the full-scale adventure, was set for spring 1943, but provision existed for a lesser attack in the fall of 1942. The latter, designated SLEDGEHAMMER, was intended either to exploit a German setback or ease German pressure in the U.S.S.R. theater. The American forces needed to accomplish this cross-Channel strategy were set in motion towards the United Kingdom under a build-up plan coded BOLERO.

In June the BOLERO plan was reaffirmed in Roosevelt-Churchill conversations. However, it was stressed that BOLERO was flexible, that it not only was flexible enough to provide against any developments on the Russian front but also did not preclude the mounting of an operation against French North Africa. Late in July ROUND-UP was definitely abandoned. In its stead TORCH, the African invasion, would be undertaken.

President Roosevelt is generally credited with inspiring much of the North African strategy; moreover the British Chiefs of Staff had always exhibited a definite reluctance to embark on a continental invasion. The U. S. Joint Chiefs of Staff, on the other hand, had been heartily in favor of ROUND-UP, had stressed its advantages over TORCH, and had labeled the latter "defensive, encircling." As will appear, high-placed American officers, and especially air officers, were to retain a preference for ROUND-UP and its corollaries, even after TORCH had broken into North Africa.

The Combined Chiefs of Staff laid down the fundamentals of the operation in August. "Firm and mutually supported lodgments" were to be established in the Oran-Algiers-Tunis area on the Mediterranean coast and in the Casablanca area on the Atlantic coast. From these lodgments control was to be extended over French North Africa with the primary object of driving against the rear of the Axis forces in the Western Desert. An amphibious assault in the Tunis area was given over because of the proximity of "Bomb Alley"--the Sardinia-Sicily-Tunis triangle dominated by Axis air forces. In order to guard against hostile action from Spanish territory cutting the life line through the Strait of Gibraltar, after the landings preparations were to be made for a possible invasion of Spanish Morocco.

General Eisenhower submitted a plan which differed in important aspects from the operation outlined in the guiding CCS directive. Generally speaking, the modifications looked towards throwing the weight of the assault farther east (landings at Oran, Algiers, and Bone) with a view to a more rapid advance on Tunis and towards chancing Spanish hostility to the extent of abandoning the Casablanca landing. The plan did indicate, however, that studies were in progress for a descent by sea on Spanish Morocco, if emergency action were required before the Oran forces, charged also with the capture of Casablanca, could consolidate on the land-ward side.

Although they granted General Eisenhower's contention that forces at hand were insufficient to carry out the original directive, the U. S. Joint Chiefs of Staff refused to take the logistical risk of hostile action closing the sea line through Gibraltar before the landline from Casablanca to Oran had been secured. They argued, therefore, that the Casablanca landings were essential and they won their point despite Eisenhower's conviction that the needs of the West Coast would spread his forces too thinly and allow the Germans entry to Tunisia where their build-up would be more rapid than that of the Allies.

Three task forces were initially to descend on French North Africa. The Eastern Assault Force, mixed British and American, was to take Algiers, whereupon the British First Army would be brought in to secure Tunisia, and operate desertwards against Rommel. American troops of the Center (Oran) Task Force and the Western (Casablanca) Task Force were to link after the attainment of their initial objectives and prepare, as the Fifth Army, for a possible thrust into Spanish Morocco. If action to secure Spanish Morocco were necessary before the Fifth Army could be consolidated, a Northern Task Force would sail from England for an attack on the Tangier-Ceuta area. This project was coded BACKBONE. Thus the primary prospective area of action of the American ground forces lay in the neighborhood of the Strait of Gibraltar and not near the Sicilian narrows. It remains to set forth the projected disposition of the American air contingent.

The land-based Allied air forces which went down to Africa in support of TORCH went as two separate air commands--separate as to tasks and areas of responsibility and operation. This arrangement is reflected in the names assigned: Eastern Air Command and Western Air Command. The Western Air Command was the Twelfth Air Force.

The British Eastern Air Command under Air Marshal Sir William Welsh, with headquarters at Algiers, was to be generally responsible for cooperation with the Eastern Assault Force and the First Army in the drive for Tunis. The Twelfth Air Force, commanded by Brig. Gen. James H. Doolittle, after giving such aid as was possible to the Center and Western Task Forces in their landings, would find its main task to be cooperation with the American Fifth Army.

The Twelfth, however, with projected headquarters at Oran, was by no means merely the air watch set over Spanish Morocco, for its assignment to the western area was not so exclusive as that of the ground forces. In the TORCH plan it was stated: "from the air point of view, the whole North African theater must be regarded as one." Moreover, the Twelfth was not only considerably larger than the Eastern Air Command but boasted the only long-range bombers, escort fighters, and transports destined for the theater. As might be expected, then, Allied Force Headquarters (AFHQ) contemplated reinforcing one command from the other and concentrating air strength in any part of the theater. The Twelfth would not sit on its hands pending Spanish developments, but its separation from the Eastern Air Command was explicit.

In its immediate impact upon North Africa, the Twelfth functioned as two air task forces, command of which led upward to ground task force commanders under general supervision of AFHQ. This arrangement was well suited to cooperation with the widely separated landings at Oran and Casablanca and to possible operations prior to the time when the Western and Center Task Forces would establish contact. Appreciation of this fact affords an entry to the tangled subject of Twelfth Air Force organization subsequent to the cessation of French resistance.

As laid out in August 1942, the Twelfth Air Force was to consist of a fighter, a bomber, and a service command and about 700 aircraft.

This force was to be organized and trained in England, its nucleus contributed by the Eighth Air Force. Although conclusive evidence cannot be brought to bear, it is likely that the Twelfth as above outlined was destined for the Casablanca area, in accordance with the old JUPITER-GYMNAST conception by which British forces were committed within the Mediterranean and American forces mainly on the west coast. Apparently, however, the USAAF very soon relieved the RAF of the burden of cooperating with the Oran forces and turned the Twelfth Air Force proper (fighter, bomber, and service commands) to that assignment. At any rate, in September the XII Air Support Command was organized to take over the other function of aiding the Western Task Force in its descent upon Casablanca.

XII Air Support Command, under Brig. Gen. John K. Cannon, approximately doubled the American air contingent for TORCH; it comprised a bomb wing (5th) and a fighter wing (7th), and in all respects was a complete air force. In fact, some of the plans gave it more aircraft than Twelfth Air Force proper. Moreover, even after Headquarters, Twelfth Air Force was established in Africa, the plan contemplated that XII ASC was still to operate under the Western Task Force commander. Indeed, General Doolittle did not assume command of this ad hoc air task force until two weeks after TORCH landed in Africa.

Chapter II
THE RACE FOR TUNIS

Prelude to Tunisia

In the late evening of 23 October 1942 Gen. Sir Harold Alexander's artillery opened on the German and Italian lines at El Alamein and by 3 November the former occupants were in full, if not disorganized, retreat from Egypt. The eastern claw of a great pincers had struck the Axis establishment in Africa. Back in England, the church bells, previously limited to providing warning of a German invasion, rang out the desert victory. Five days later, on 8 November, the heartened Allied public was treated to coordinated strategy on the grand scale: Allied task forces went ashore on the beaches flanking Oran, Algiers, and Casablanca in French North Africa. The western claw had shown itself.

At the outset, the great amphibious venture enjoyed more good fortune than an ordinary military operation has any right to expect. The secret of TORCH had been so well kept that the Axis had only a vague uneasiness in regard to North Africa, an uneasiness which expended itself on the neighborhood of Dakar. The armadas converging on Gibraltar and Casablanca were a U-boat commander's dream, but the bulk of the German Atlantic pack took off after a small England-bound convoy out of Sierra Leone and left the sea paths clear.[1] And although surf on the Moroccan coast has been known to break in 30-foot waves, particularly in autumnal storms, General Patton's men landed on a day reportedly the calmest in 68 years.

In its assault phase, the TORCH operation had not allowed great opportunity for the employment of land-based aviation. Nevertheless, the Twelfth Air Force had brought Spitfires of the 31st Fighter Group into Oran's Tafaraoui airdrome by the afternoon of D-day. Flown in from Gibraltar, these fighters added materially to the discomfiture of the French defenders. Over on the West Coast, a similar role had been projected for the 33d Fighter Group, carrier-borne on the U.S.S. Chenango, but the French put up their most determined local resistance at the approaches to the Port Lyautey airdrome and the P-40's did not fly off until the ground arm, aided by the U. S. Navy and its aircraft, had just about convinced the French that their case was hopeless. In addition, the 60th Troop Carrier Group had flown a D-day paratroop mission against the La Senia and Tafaraoui airfields at Oran---a mission which, for a variety of reasons ended unhappily in a dry lake bed.[2]

By 11 November, with the armistice at Casablanca, French resistance in Algeria and Morocco had come to an end. Troops of the Center and Western forces, scattered from Arzeu to Mazagan, began pushing out for a junction in French Morocco. When they made contact on the 24th at Taza, a preliminary plan had already been agreed upon for concerted action by French and Americans in the event of an attack from Spanish Morocco.[3] More urgent events were underway in the east, where the British First Army, abetted by American troops from both the Oran and Algiers forces, was racing to eject the Germans and Italians from Tunisia.

For a time after the armistice, the Twelfth Air Force chiefly occupied itself in setting up housekeeping. Its supplies poured ashore, at Arzeu, Mers-el-Kebir, Safi, Fedala, and Port Lyautey and, after their harbors were cleared, at Oran and Casablanca. Truck service, utilizing many rejuvenated French vehicles, hauled equipment from the docks to the newly captured airdromes. Ground echelons tramped through the strange countryside to their stations, and soon a vigorous trade with the natives in which GI shirts and mattress covers, eggs, tangerines, and chickens became staple.[4]

According to plan, XII Fighter Command, XII Bomber Command, 51st Troop Carrier Wing, and Headquarters, Twelfth Air Force established themselves at Oran. Airfields were fairly numerous in the vicinity, but most of them partook more of the nature of landing grounds and only one, Tafaraoui, possessed a paved runway, a detail soon to assume considerable importance. As Air Corps troops by the thousands converged on the major bases of La Senia and Tafaraoui, a congestion of no mean proportions arose. General Cannon, in Morocco, had a little more latitude--not so many men and more fields: Port Lyautey, Cazes (at Casablanca), Mediouna, Rabat, Rabat Sale, Meknes, and Marrakech.[5]

The build-up of the Twelfth proceeded rapidly. Besides the 33d Fighter Group, by the 19th of November XII Air Support Command had received 35 replacement P-40's catapulted from the British auxiliary carrier Archer, a half-dozen B-25's of the 310th Group, and a number of C-47's of the 62d Troop Carrier Group. By the same date, the USAAF in Algeria boasted the 1st, 14th, 31st, and 52d Fighter Groups, the 15th

Light Bombardment Squadron (DB-7's), the 60th and 64th Troop Carrier Groups, and two B-17 squadrons of the 97th Group. The build-up was the more impressive in view of the congestion at the Gibraltar airdrome, through which many of these aircraft had to be routed. Of all these, the 51st Troop Carrier Wing's C-47's, under Col. Paul L. Williams, took on the most immediate tactical importance.[6]

The Contribution of the C-47's

Speed was the essence of the plan to seize Tunisia, for a bare hundred miles from the big prizes of Bizerte and Tunis lay Sicily, the great Axis base. On 9 November, the day after the Allied landings in the west, three-motored Ju-52 transports had landed at Tunis' El Aouina airdrome, without opposition from the French. On that same day, Gen. K.A.N. Anderson arrived in Algiers to take command of the eastward push, his principal instruments being the British First Army and the RAF's Eastern Air Command. Preparations against Tunisia got underway while fighting still raged at Oran and Casablanca.

General Anderson found himself 400 miles from Tunis. He had, perhaps, a month of good weather to make contact with and smash the Axis build-up before the heavy winter rains of the Tunisian north coast would set in. The intervening country was broken by mountains and was poor in highways and railroads. A single narrow-gauge railroad ran from Casablanca on to Tunis; its condition may be judged from the fact that shortly after the Allied occupation the fast passenger train from Oran to Algiers, 200 miles away, negotiated the distance in 38 hours. In such circumstances, an orthodox land advance was out of the question. The plans called for the rapid seizure of successive ports, troops to be rushed forward by landing craft, motor transport, and troop-carrier aircraft. To cover the advance the coastal airdromes had to be secured for the use of Eastern Air Command's Spitfires.[7]

At the outset, a spell of rough sea cost the Allies two precious days. At dawn on 11 November the British 36th Brigade Group went ashore unopposed at the port of Bougie, 100 miles east of Algiers, but an attempted landing at Djidjelli, about 40 miles further down the coast, was frustrated by a heavy swell. Before the airdrome at Djidjelli could be secured Bomb Alley became a reality: the GAF sank three U. S. combat loaders in Bougie harbor and damaged the British carrier *Argus*, whose aircraft, abetted by fighters at extreme range from Maison Blanche at Algiers, were covering the operation. The next Allied objectives were Philippeville and Bone. Against the latter, a major port 150 miles east of Bougie, American troop carrier aircraft were employed.[8]

The design for using paratroops to seize the airfields on the way to the Tunis tip went back at least as far as Maj. Gen. Mark Clark's famous submarine trip in late October, at which time he conferred near Algiers with Gen. Charles Mast and other Frenchmen sympathetic to the Allies. At this meeting assurances were given that transport aircraft could land unopposed at the Oran airdromes and at those in the vicinity of Bone. Allied Force Headquarters at once made plans to the effect that the 60th Troop Carrier Group would come in at La Senia from England without jumping its passengers and be ready immediately for a movement to Bone and a subsequent parachute descent in Tunisia. Unfortunately, the transports, proceeding on this plan, found the French at La Senia not at all friendly: AA opened on the C-47's, Dewoitine fighters shot several down, and many of the aircraft were damaged in landing on the dry bed of the Sebkra d'Oran. They could not be made ready in time for Bone.[9]

On the afternoon of D-day, General Eisenhower's CP at Gibraltar requested that 39 troop carriers of the 64th Group be sent with British paratroops to Algiers from the United Kingdom. The planes staged through St. Eval from Hurn on the 9th and at 2300 departed with the 3d Paratroop Battalion for Gibraltar. Thirty-four of them made Algiers early on the morning of the 11th, to be greeted by antiaircraft fire which wounded two men. Next morning 26 C-47's took off and with escorting fighters flew along the Mediterranean to the Duzerville airdrome, six miles southeast of Bone, where two companies of the 3d Battalion were successfully dropped. All of the transports were back on Maison Blanche by noon.[10]

At Bone itself, two destroyers had landed British commandos at dawn. These came in unopposed, but on the night of the 12th, Axis planes bombed the airfield so heavily as to threaten to make it untenable. The situation was relieved when the 64th's C-47's, with P-38 escort, made two flights into Duzerville, ferrying antiaircraft guns and aviation gasoline. Such uses of air transport were of tremendous value as the slim Allied forces stabbed towards Tunis.[11]

Meanwhile, the Allied commanders were laboring to galvanize the hesitant Tunisian French into action. Admiral Darlan and General Giraud issued orders for resistance to the Germans, and Giraud, with General Juin, prepared to make a reconnaissance of the Tunisian border. By 13 November, Blade Force, the British armored unit destined to be the core of the eastward dash, had come by sea into Bone and an American tank-destroyer battalion had been ordered in from Oran to bolster the ill-equipped French. On the 15th, elements of the British 36th Brigade occupied Tabarka on the coast, only 60 miles from Tunis, and American paratroops were dropping far inland.[12]

After its D-day adventures at Oran, the Paratroop Task Force (60th Troop Carrier Group and 2d Battalion, 503d Parachute Infantry) took some time to reassemble and refit. On the 10th, operational control of the paratroops was transferred to the British First Army commander and the unit was ordered to Algiers. By the 12th, 25 C-47's of the 60th and 300 of the paratroopers were at Maison Blanche, ready for action, and two days later, Col. Edson D. Raff and Maj. Martin E. Wanamaker, commanding the transports, were called to Allied headquarters and assigned a mission for the following day.[13]

The objective was out near Tunisia, Youks-les-Bains airfield. It lay 10 miles east of the important town of Tebessa, a road hub and terminus of railroads leading from Tunis, Souk Ahras, and Constantine. The airfield itself was about 100 miles south of Bone and 150 southwest of Tunis. Intelligence about the area was meager and uncertain, especially as to the reaction of the local French forces to parachute troops, and German and Italian patrols reportedly in the vicinity might even be in possession of the field. Despite these variables, Colonel Raff and Major Wanamaker hurriedly made plans.

At 0730 on 15 November, 20 C-47's of the 60th, loaded with 350 paratroopers and their supplies, left Maison Blanche. Six British Spitfires escorted the flight along the coast to Djidjelli, where six Hurricanes were picked up. Thence the route lay south and east. Dirty weather forced both transports and escort onto instruments, but the formation was successfully led to the drop zone and at 0945 the paratroops were dropped en masse from 400 feet or less. The landing pattern was perfect, Colonel Raff allowing himself to be quoted to the effect that it was the most successful jump he had ever made. Two enemy planes had been sighted near the drop zone, but they did not attack. The return trip, over the same route, passed uneventfully except that one C-47 developed engine trouble and landed safely at Djidjelli. The rest of the formation made Algiers by 1215.[14]

The same day's weather had got the better of the 64th Troop Carrier Group, which attempted unsuccessfully to jump British paratroops at Souk el Arba airdrome, in the valley of the Medjerda about 90 miles from Tunis. On the 16th, however, the mission was successfully accomplished. Thirty-two C-47's took off from Maison Blanche at 0700, accompanied by 18 fighters. As the formation passed Bone, enemy planes could be seen bombing and strafing its airfield, but approximately 500 paratroopers were dropped on the Souk el Arba drome and all the C-47's returned to base.[15]

The Twelfth Moves Eastward

In an effort to gain and defend a Tunisian bridgehead, the Axis was pouring in men and weapons from Sicily. On 17 November the hostile establishment at Tunis was estimated at up to a thousand men, with 4,000 more over at Bizerte, where the Ju-52's averaged more than 50 landings a day at Sidi Ahmed. This force mustered some medium tanks, and its German and Italian infantry was strong in antiaircraft and anti-tank guns. Based on the airdromes at Tunis and Bizerte were about 150 fighters and dive bombers, including some Italian pursuits, which had not yet heavily attacked the approaching Allies. The destructive raids against Bone and Bougie had been mainly undertaken by long-range German bombers from Sicily and Sardinia.

After prolonged indecision, the French garrisons in Tunisia came over to the Allies, General Barre having broken off the negotiations with Von Arnim which had gone on ever since the Germans set foot in the country. It was agreed that the French troops under Generals Barre, Juin, and Koeltz would observe and harass by guerrilla tactics, the German advance from the bridgehead. Their equipment and morale rendered a more positive role impracticable. On 16 November, the French drove off German patrols at Oued Zarga and Mateur on the main roads leading out of Tunis and Bizerte. By the 17th, however, the Germans had occupied Mateur and had made contact with the British at Djebel Abiod on the coast road and the French at Medjez-el-Bab. In the south, Colonel Raff's paratroopers established friendly relations with the local French, occupied Gafsa airfield, 80 miles southeast of Tebessa, and began to clash with Italian patrols moving inland from Sfax and Gabes. The elements of a definite front were present.[16]

Despite the weaknesses of the French, General Eisenhower hoped that they could be used, in effect, to bluff the Germans. He cabled General Clark on 17 November urging that General Giraud order the French to advance everywhere, make a great show of activity, spread rumors about oncoming and formidable forces of British and Americans, and generally induce the enemy to tie himself down to local defense of Tunis and Bizerte. The Germans, however, seized the initiative. After two ultimatums, Von Arnim to Barre, the French at Medjez-el-Bab were attacked on the 18th and 19th with infantry, tanks, artillery, and dive bombers. No air support could be given them; they suffered 25 per cent casualties and retired to Oued Zarga. A German attack against the British at Djebel Abiod, however, was held.[17]

Except for the not inconsiderable contributions of its troop-carrier aircraft, the entry of the Twelfth Air Force into this struggle was spontaneous rather than planned, in the sense that on paper the support of the British First Army devolved primarily upon the Eastern

Air Command. However, by 19 November Doolittle (to become a major general on the next day) was at Algiers consulting with the British concerning the eastward extension of his forces, and by 28 November Headquarters, Twelfth Air Force was no longer at Tafaraoui but was listed as at Standard Oil Building, Boulevard Victor Hugo, Algiers.[18]

In order to fulfill the twin commitments of guarding against an Axis move from Spain or its Moroccan colony and of giving all possible aid to the British in Tunisia, General Doolittle soon came to the conclusion that it was necessary to revamp his air force. XII Air Support Command, with its subordinate fighter and bomber wings had followed the Western Task Force into French Morocco. XII Fighter Command, XII Bomber Command, and 51st Troop Carrier Wing had been initially established at Oran. By 19 November, however, the commander was turning over in his mind an organization plan more suited to the demands likely to be made upon him.

He visualized composite organizations, small air forces, each with its requirements of pursuit and bombardment. XII Air Support Command would temporarily remain at Casablanca and later move to Oran, to the anticipated headquarters of the American Fifth Army. Meanwhile XII Fighter Command would function at Oran and XII Bomber Command in the battle area east of Algiers. General Doolittle was preparing for a conference with the RAF as a result of which he hoped to have an easterly sector assigned to American units. Although the above plan was never promulgated precisely as outlined, it contained the germs of future Twelfth Air Force organization.

Actually, the tactical situation seems to have governed organization in the early days. The 31st and 52d Fighter Groups, first into Africa, were initially left at Oran and designated as reserves for the Eastern Air Command, logically enough, since the Spitfires could be easily maintained by the RAF. As additional American units came in, they were generally moved via Algiers to join in the fray.[19]

First unit to draw blood in Africa was the 97th Heavy Bombardment Group, which already had a famous first to its credit--the raid of 17 August 1942 on Rouen which inaugurated VIII Bomber Command's operations against Europe. In the absence of medium bombardment, which was delayed by adverse conditions including the rough weather over the North Atlantic route, the 97th had been ordered down to Africa much earlier than the TORCH schedules contemplated. On 10 November, the flight echelon of its 340th Squadron left Polebrook, England, for Gibraltar, remained there for two days, and on the 13th came into Maison Blanche. By the 15th, the men were "promoting" transportation and pouring gasoline from five-gallon flimsies in preparation for their first raid.

On the 16th six B-17's took off, unescorted, for Bizerte. From 6,500 feet, they dropped British bombs on the Sidi Ahmed airdrome, destroying several aircraft on the ground. They also knocked down one of the Me-109's which rose to intercept. All six returned, and their flak holes were repaired on the following day with tin cans and adhesive tape. By the 18th, P-38's became available for escort when the two squadrons of the 14th Fighter Group came into Maison Blanche from Tafaraoui, after flying nonstop from England. The Luftwaffe greeted the new arrivals with a raid on the airfield during which seven P-38's were damaged. On the 19th, the 97th went out again, accompanied by the Lightnings. At El Aouina airdrome at Tunis the bombers burned eight planes on the ground and, according to General Doolittle, probably damaged 30 more. Me-109's came up but did not attack, although one exchanged shots with a P-38. That evening the enemy again pounded Algiers.[20]

On the evening of the 20th the enemy outdid himself. A force reported as from 30 to 60 Ju-87's and Ju-88's, probably from Sardinia, carried out the raid, hitting at both the harbor and Maison Blanche. On the airfield, the enemy scattered thousands of sharp, pyramid-shaped spikes, which subsequently wrecked several Allied fighters by blowing their tires, and booby traps in the form of fountain pens, wallets and watches. On the ground his score was impressive: an entire RAF photo reconnaissance (PR) unit, four Spits, three Beaufighters, two P-38's and a B-17. No interception could be made as no Allied fighters possessed aerial interception equipment. These raids worried General Eisenhower, who feared a concentrated German effort on Algiers. Targets abounded: Maison Blanche and Blida, packed with British and American aircraft; the crowded harbor; the vital railways, docks, and meager signal communications; and the civilian population, generally sympathetic to the Allies but inclined to feel that the Allies had brought the war to their doorsteps. Requests for aid immediately went forward--to London for night fighters and to the CCS for radar and balloon units.[21]

In the battle for Tunisia the Germans and Italians had the initial advantage of air power based on permanent bases in Sardinia and Sicily and on the all-weather fields at El Aouina and Sidi Ahmed on the African mainland. The Allies, on the other hand, were forced to use every landing strip between Oran and the front lines. Inevitably, aircraft accumulated at the major bases. On 18 November General Spaatz arrived at Maison Blanche and departed with the impression that this base at Algiers lacked organization and was too far forward and too exposed for heavy bombers. On his return to Gibraltar on the 19th he went over the situation with General Eisenhower.[22]

On that day the command post at Gibraltar dispatched a cable to Air Marshal Welsh and General Clark, suggesting a plan for the employment of American air units and probably reflecting General Spaatz's sentiments. The B-17's were to be removed to Tafaraoui where maintenance would be easier than at Algiers; they could pick up P-38 escort at Maison Blanche, or at a more forward airdrome, and their range would still permit raids on Tunis and Bizerte. Apparently, the suggestion was not immediately followed. General Clark wired back on the 21st that he agreed with Air Marshal Welsh, General Doolittle, and Brig. Gen. Howard Craig (AFHQ's deputy assistant chief of staff for air) that the B-17's could operate better from Algiers than Tafaraoui.

Plans were actually underway to send the rest of the 97th to Maison Blanche, where the ground echelons of the 319th Medium Bombardment Group were doubling in B-17 maintenance. As General Clark wrote the wire, however, he mentioned that another raid on Algiers was in progress.[23]

This raid of the night of the 21st destroyed another of the 97th's B-17's. The group had been over El Aouina during the day and all of its flight echelons had finally arrived at Maison Blanche. Evidently a hasty decision to move them out of Algiers was made, for on the 22d the heavies went back to Oran. Thenceforth, until mid-December, they operated mostly from Tafaraoui, where as the famous rhyme had it the mud was "deep and gooey."[24]

In his letter of 19 November, General Doolittle had mentioned that he had scheduled for that day a meeting with the RAF, as a result of which he hoped to have a forward sector assigned to the Twelfth Air Force. Whether or not the meeting took place on the 19th, it was Air Marshal Welsh who chose the Tebessa region as a forward base area for the Twelfth; and the units that went down as a result of his decision were the forerunners of the formidable XII Air Support Command of later months. On 22 November, the 14th Fighter Group moved to Youks-les-Bains, the airdrome seized a week before by Colonel Raff's paratroopers; its two squadrons proceeded to fly two strafing missions to the east the same day. The workhorse C-47's had paved the way by flying in necessary supplies and equipment, and for a long time the units at Youks were to be largely dependent on air transport.[25]

Shortly after the P-38's had begun operations from Youks, the 15th Light Bombardment Squadron (DB-7's) was sent down from Algiers, coming under the jurisdiction of XII Fighter Command and Col. Thayer S. Olds, CO of the 14th Group. The 15th had had an interesting background in the European theater. First AAF combat unit to arrive in England, it had been intended as a night fighter squadron using British equipment but was reconverted to light bombardment. Some of its personnel had participated in the raid of 4 July 1942 against airdromes in Holland, the first in ETO in which American flyers participated. After a period of operations under VIII Bomber Command, the unit was given over to the Twelfth. On 15 November, it left England for Oran, barely escaped disaster in a front off the Spanish coast, and came in safely after almost nine hours of flying. When the unit departed Maison Blanche for Youks, each DB-7 carried two 500-lb. bombs for immediate operations.[26]

With the 14th Group out in the Tebessa mountains, the mission of escorting B-17's fell to the P-38's of the 1st Fighter Group. The 1st had made the long overwater flight from England with the loss of only one pilot--another was interned at Lisbon--and its complete flight echelon had reached Tafaraoui by 15 November. On 21 November, the Group was at Nouvion, 40 miles east of Oran.[27]

The Drive for Tunis

While the Twelfth Air Force was moving into the battle, the Allied ground forces were concentrating in the forward area, their headquarters attempting to bring order out of a considerable intermixture of French and British units. By 23 November an arrangement had been reached by which all troops north of the line Le Kef-Zaghouan were to be under British command, those to the south under French, the latter with the function of protecting the right of General Anderson's advance. The push opened on the 24th, with the line of Tebourba-Mateur as the first objective---the ultimate plan being to drive a wedge between Tunis and Bizerte, capture the former, and hem the Germans in on the northernmost tip of Tunisia. Almost all Twelfth Air Force activity was in support of this operation, the British assigning the targets.[28]

Progress was at first steady. On the morning of the 26th, the British 78th Division flanked and captured Medjez-el-Bab while Blade Force advanced to a point midway between Mateur and Tebourba. On the night of the 26th Tebourba itself was taken, and counterattacks employing tanks and dive bombers were successfully beaten off. Djedeida, from which the ridge of the Kasba at Tunis could be seen only 16 miles away, was reached by the 28th. On its landing ground occurred an unusual encounter. An American tank rumbling down the slopes back of the town noticed Ju-87's, the dive bombers whose attacks were becoming increasingly troublesome, disappearing behind a hill. The tank commander upon investigation found himself on a lightly defended, Stuka-packed airdrome. With relish succeeding tanks went on to the attack, destroyed gas and ammunition dumps, ran down pilots under treads, and wrecked 33 Ju-87's.[29]

By 22 November the Eastern Air Command had moved a Spitfire squadron into Souk el Arba, about 70 miles from the front, which was to be the RAF's most forward base during the crucial period which followed. Night operations against the bridgehead were begun by a squadron of British Bisleys (Blenheim V's). To counter the enemy's determined attacks against the important supply port of Bone the 2d Squadron of the U. S. 52d Fighter Group was sent to reinforce the RAF at the covering airdrome. The 2d remained at Bone until 4 January 1943, patrolling over the harbor, participating in sweeps into Tunisia, and escorting Hurribombers. At times, this unit was altogether out of touch with the Twelfth Air Force, a not unusual occurrence in the hectic early days when everything was subordinated to the task of smashing the Axis lodgment.[30]

Early Allied bombing, whether by Bisleys, B-17's, or DB-7's, was directed against the principal Tunisian airdromes in hope of crippling the enemy's air power--witness the first three missions flown by the 97th. After the B-17's had been established at Tafaraoui, the 97th was ordered to attack the Elmas airdrome in southern Sardinia, just outside the city of Cagliari, from which the enemy was mounting attacks on the Algerian ports and the Allied convoys, which latter by 16 November were also running a gantlet of nearly 30 submarines operating in the Western Mediterranean and its Atlantic approaches. Fourteen B-17's took off on 23 November at 0640 led by Col. Joseph H. Atkinson, CO of the 97th. One turned back with oxygen failure in the ball turret, but the others met 27 P-38's of the 1st Fighter Group over Mostaganem and proceeded towards the target. Two hundred and fifty miles from

Elmas the formation turned back in the face of a violent subtropical front.[31]

On the 24th Bizerte harbor was the target, and the B-17's got to within 100 miles before bad weather again forced them back. The weathermen were having serious trouble with their forecasts because of the mass of enemy territory to the north. Abortives from erroneous weather reports were later lessened by the practice of sending P-38's on early-morning weather reconnaissance over the general target area. On the 28th the bombers provoked a minor air battle over Bizerte. Thirty-seven B-17's of the 97th and the newly arrived 301st went out after the airport and docks, their usual P-38 escorts being mudded in at Nouvion. Hits were scored on both targets, heavy flak was encountered, and 10 enemy aircraft were claimed as destroyed. Two B-17's were shot down by the enemy fighters, a mixture of Me-109's and FW-190's.[32]

From Tafaraoui the B-17's were operating at close to maximum range. The distance to Bizerte was almost 600 miles. Of course, if the bombers ran short of gas on the return trip, they could land at Maison Blanche or other friendly airdromes east of Oran. Escort was picked up at Maison Blanche, where one squadron of the 1st Fighter Group was available by 27 November. Two days earlier the 1st had sent another of its squadrons, the 94th, down to reinforce the 14th Group at Youks-les-Bains.

In the first week of December, the Twelfth Air Force was able to move four squadrons of its B-17's forward to the Algiers area, where the range was more comfortable. On the 5th the rear echelon of XII Bomber Command was ordered to send, with minimum personnel, 18 B-17's of the 97th to Blida, about 30 miles southeast of Algiers, and a like number of the 301st to Maison Blanche. The next forward movement waited upon the availability of the new desert airdrome at Biskra.[33]

Meanwhile, the remote units at Youks were fighting their own air war. On its first day of operations the 14th Fighter Group shot down a Ju-88 and an Italian bomber. According to an unconfirmed report it had a field day out near Gabes on the 24th, destroying two Ju-88's and seven Italian transports in the air and five unidentified transports and a single-engine fighter on the ground--all at the cost of a damaged plane and an injured pilot. The performance of the P-38F against the Ju-88 proved to be consistently good. Particularly impressed by it was a former intelligence officer of the U. S. 31st Group who had been familiar with the Spitfire V's efforts at intercepting the crack German bomber over England. The Spit had the advantage of good radar and plenty of time to intercept, yet it not only experienced difficulty in catching the Ju-88 but was often shot down by the latter's counterfire. Over Youks and Tebessa, on the other hand, the P-38's, with normally only visual warning, repeatedly overtook and destroyed the bombers on their way back to the coast. It was true, however, that the Ju-88's in Africa carried less firepower.[34]

At this time, the Allies were represented in southern Tunisia by six French battalions and Colonel Raff's paratroop battalion, reinforced.

These units patrolled over a wide area east of Tebessa, protecting the extreme right flank of the First Army in the north. The American air units at Youks, however, found their primary targets in the area affected by the main push--the drive towards Tunis and Bizerte, although at times conflicts developed between the requirements of the two sectors. By 27 November, however, the Youks aircraft were made available to the British 78th Division, operating forward of Hedjez-el-Bab.[35]

On 28 November the Allied forces pushing at Djedeida and Mateur seemed about to break through the crust of the German defense, despite demolitions, mines, booby traps, and intensive dive bombing and level bombing by Ju-87's and Ju-88's. The sitrep for that date was particularly optimistic; it described heavy German tank losses, Djedeida being cleaned up, Pont du Fahs evacuated, and enemy supplies abandoned and burned. At this point, a paratroop attack was ordered for 29 November against the area southwest of Tunis.[36]

The object of the attack has been variously stated, but the principal objective was evidently the airdrome at Oudna, 10 miles from Tunis. After capturing the field and destroying stores and aircraft there, the paratroopers were to threaten the southern approaches to Tunis by infiltrating between enemy strong-points. Eventually, the force would link up with the advancing Allied army.[37]

The drop was made at Depienne, 10 miles north of Pont du Fahs. Forty-four transports, 26 of the 62d Troop Carrier Group and 18 of the

64th, carrying 530 men of the second battalion of the British parachute brigade, participated in the mission under the personal command of Colonel Williams. By 1230 on the 29th the last C-47 had taken off to join the formation over Maison Blanche. Escort initially consisted of 4 Hurricanes and 8 P-38's; at Le Kef 14 Spitfires were added. Despite a stiff tail wind and a ragged formation, the troop carriers arrived at the chosen point and dropped their passengers between 1330 and 1400 hours. No air opposition developed and the C-47's all came safely back to base.[38]

Not so the paratroops. Five days later the remainder got back to the Allied lines--lines that had not advanced as planned. Oudna airdrome had been heavily defended, and tanks and armored cars had put in an appearance; three hundred dead and wounded would not return. This ended the last major paratroop operation in the North African campaign.[39]

Stalemate

The advance on Tunis was in fact stalled. Djedeida, it turned out, had not been completely occupied and the British 36th Brigade was still involved northwest of Mateur. The largest factor in the check was German front-line air superiority which manifested itself in intensive bombing of the Allied troops. Moreover, it is probable that Axis troops were by now at least as numerous as the scanty contingents the Allies had thrown forward. The long and vulnerable Allied line of communication, over which French troops and stores were also moving, was taking its toll.

The GAF and its satellite IAF were excellently disposed to support the Axis defense. In Tunisia, they enjoyed the use of the concrete runways of Sidi Ahmed and El Aouina and of coastal airdromes to the south, at Sfax, Sousse, and Gabes. Moreover, their ground arm held the Tunisian plains of which large areas were usable, almost without preparation, as landing grounds. The numerous Sicilian airdromes lay only a half-hour away.

From Sicily and Sardinia the Luftwaffe operated against the Allied LOC at Bone, Bougie, and Algiers. Its fleets of air transports shuttled between Sicily and Bizerte with men and supplies, and AA and radar soon appeared in the Tunis-Bizerte area to aid the FW-190's and Me-109's in defense of the ports. Of most immediate tactical importance, however, was the role of the obsolescent but numerous Ju-87, the Stuka. Abetted by Me-109's, operating as fighter-bombers, and by the Ju-88's, this traditional Luftwaffe weapon claimed much of the credit for stopping the Allied advance. The Germans were able to base the Stuka at El Aouina, barely a score of miles from the front at Djedeida, and, since the plane was light, at landing grounds and in open fields just beyond the range of Allied artillery. Army calls for support, made by voice radio in the clear, could be answered within five to 10 minutes.

The Eastern Air Command and the Twelfth could have emphasized the Ju-87's obsolescence, as the Allied air units in the Middle East had done, had they been able to get at it. Unfortunately, their ground arm had seized for the most part no more than the Tunisian hill country in which airdromes were scarce. In late November, just three forward fields were available: Bone, 120 miles from the lines, Youks, about 150 miles away, and the landing ground at Souk el Arba, 70 miles back.

The Spitfires from Souk el Arba and Bone, with their inferior range, could remain over the battle area for only five to 10 minutes. On their appearance, the German air pulled out over the Gulf of Tunis or landed its Ju-87's at forward landing grounds and parked them under trees. When the sweep had disappeared over the western hills the bombers resumed their work. The P-38's from Youks found the range more convenient, but there were not enough of them for the job. Over the Allied fighters, which had to escort paratroops and bombers and cover the shipping to Bone, the Me-109's and FW-190's consistently enjoyed numerical superiority. On sweeps over the battle area, the Spits and P-38's frequently were hard put to defend themselves, let alone scatter the enemy bombers.[40]

The last week in November saw Generals Eisenhower and Clark at the front, and on the 29th the Commander in Chief radioed back ordering an air attack on the North Quay at Bizerte. On that day, Tafaraoui mud had already canceled one expedition to Bizerte, but on the 30th the North Quay was visited with results described as fair. Of 24 B-17's out of Tafaraoui, only nine managed to bomb through a break in the clouds. Meanwhile, in an attempt to restrict hostile air activity, Air Marshal Welsh had determined upon a further series of attacks on enemy airfields. On the 1st of December, the 97th Group proceeded to implement this policy by effectively bombing El Aouina. Thirteen Fortresses, escorted by 24 P-38's, dropped 65 x 100-lb. and 65 x 300-lb. bombs with bursts visible on the hangar line and the built-up area of the field. Flak was weak and ineffective, only one Me-109 was seen and chased.[41]

Two days before, on the 28th, the mediums had made their debut with the bombing of Sfax harbor by the 319th, a group which had reached Africa only after considerable tribulation. En route to England by air it had lost planes and crews in the North Atlantic and many of the B-26's were weather-marooned on Greenland and Iceland. En route to Africa, ill fortune continued to pursue it. One day nine of its planes left England with misleading weather data; two blundered into France and were shot down over Cherbourg, Col. Alvord Rutherford, group CO, being among those lost. About 15 Marauders finally assembled for operations at Maison Blanche.[42]

Kairouan aircrome had been the primary target of the B-26's on the 28th, but no aircraft or installations of importance were observed there, so the formation turned south for Sfax. Oil tanks, warehouses, docks, and railroad yards were bombed from 1,000 feet and large fires set. In addition, several of the B-26's came down for strafing runs. This practice soon ceased after the Germans had time to bring in AA, and the mediums were eventually forced to bomb such targets from altitudes up to 12,000 feet; but on the first mission they got away with only one aircraft damaged by flak.[43]

Two days later the 319th attacked the field at Gabes. Maj. David Jones who had succeeded to command of the group, led out nine of his planes, escorted by eight P-38's. With maps covering only part of the journey, he nevertheless found the target and his planes dropped 116 x 100-lb. bombs on the airdrome, railroad junction, and yards. A concentration of light flak was encountered and one B-26 crash-landed 20 miles west of Gabes. When the crew was observed walking around, XII Fighter Command was called on for help. While two P-38's covered the operation, a DB-7 from Youks landed on the bumpy ground near the wreck. Minus one member of its customary crew, the light bomber took two of the stranded men in its nose, two in the cockpit, and four aft and got all safely away.[44]

The Youks aircraft were also participating in the assault on the GAF's fields, the 15th Squadron losing one out of three DB-7's in an attack on Gabes airdrome on the 29th. This aircraft crash-landed near Gafsa. On the same day P-38's intercepted and shot down two Me-110's north of Gabes. For the next two days the force was active in the northern sector. Fourteen P-38's took nine DB-7's up to Djedeida on the 30th, where they dropped 36 x 500-lb. bombs and scored hits on a bridge and railroad station. One P-38 did not return. The Lightnings were carrying out their usual reconnaissance and strafing missions near the coast, and on a sweep to Mateur 12 of them encountered 10 Me-109's, destroying one for the loss of one P-38. On the morning of 1 December the DB-7's bombed El Aouina, their escort knocking down one of six Me-109's found patrolling over Tunis; in the afternoon Djedeida town was attacked. On an earlier sweep over this area a dozen P-38's which had been strafing dispersed tanks were jumped by eight FW-190's. The Lightnings, caught at low level, took evasive action, but left one of their number behind.[45]

The Tunis advance had passed high tide. General Anderson had planned an offensive for 2 December to employ the newly arrived Combat Command B of the U. S. 1st Armored Division, but he was anticipated on the day before, when Von Arnim counterattacked with tanks and infantry, striking in the direction of Tebourba from the north. The much-battered Blade Force withdrew towards Tebourba and Combat Command B replaced it, alongside the British 11th Brigade.

In the early hours of 2 December, a frankly worried General Anderson radioed his appreciation of the situation. He foresaw that unless he was able to take either Tunis or Bizerte in the next few days, a temporary withdrawal was mandatory. Three factors controlled the situation: administration, the enemy's air action, and his rate of reinforcement. Normal administration had been intentionally disregarded in the race for Tunis, the army and air forces working with precarious communications and no reserve supplies. The general believed enemy air action "almost entirely" responsible for the bogging down of his advance and he recognized that for "geographical" reasons, his supporting air units could not counter the threat. Bisleys, Bostons (DB-7's), and Fortresses all had hit El Aouina on 1 December, but the limited scale of attack did not suffice. Since enemy air tactics had rendered fighter sweeps from existing airdromes ineffective, General Anderson was making arrangements for an advanced landing ground at Medjez-el-Bab. However, if Tunis or Bizerte did not soon fall, he would have to withdraw so that his overworked air could protect him. At bottom, the issue depended on the German build-up, which the British commander suspected exceeded his own. But, not satisfied with his scattered information, he asked that Brig. E. E. Mockler-Ferryman, AFHQ's G-2, be sent forward to estimate the Axis capabilities for reinforcement.[46]

Meanwhile, the Twelfth continued to hammer the airdromes. On 2 December, the DB-7's had first crack at El Aouina, the 94th Squadron of the 1st Fighter Group, by now arrived at Youks, escorting them in. Nine DB-7's bombed at 0810, and the crews reported the airfield in bad shape from the previous day's pounding. Forty minutes later a dozen B-26's of the 319th, escorted by half their number of Lightnings, took off for the same destination. Over the target at 1059, they counted about 50 enemy aircraft on the field: Ju-52's, Ju-88's, Me-109's and Me-110's. Their 215 x 100-lb. bomb load damaged 15 to 20 planes. Hangars and aircraft blazed as the B-26's turned away, to strafe flak and machine gun positions near Ariana on their way home.[47]

Sidi Ahmed and adjacent Bizerte harbor claimed the attentions of the heavies, 18 of which from the 301st left Tafaraoui at 0630 to 0650. Sixteen passed over the target shortly after 1000 hours and from 20,000 feet scored on the airdrome and its hangars and on the port's array of shipping and docks. The final attack of the day was made by B-25's of the 310th Group on their first combat mission for the Twelfth. Like the 319th, the 310th had also experienced delays in becoming operational in Africa. For one thing, a good many of its planes were used to navigate for fighter units making the overwater run from England. As a consequence, the aircraft arrived singly, and were still arriving in March 1943. Eight planes and crews had accumulated at Maison Blanche by 2 December; they took off at 1013, picked up P-38's of the 14th Group at Youks, and at 1300 bombed a reported heavy flak concentration in a wood south of Gabes. They encountered neither flak nor enemy aircraft; in fact none of the raids of the 2d reported interception.[48]

The fighters at Youks continued to perform sweeps in the battle area. Twelve were over Mateur-Djedeida on the morning of the 2d. They caught a routine German bombing mission on its way up to the front lines--eight Ju-88's with an Me-109 escort. Upon attack by the P-38's, the bombers jettisoned their loads, but one Ju-88 fell to the Lightnings, which also claimed one Me-109 probably destroyed and a Ju-88 and Me-109 damaged. Another dozen P-38's were active in the afternoon, attacking Sidi Tabet, 11 miles northwest of Tunis, one of many landing grounds the Germans were using in the area. The P-38's came in low, strafing, and destroyed two Stukas and one Me-109 on the ground. Earlier, four Lightnings on reconnaissance of Sfax and Gabes had chanced upon six Me-109's taking off from the Gabes airdrome and shot down three.[49]

The German Counterblow

On 3 December, the Germans attacked again. To the accompaniment of a lavish use of dive bombers, the 11th Brigade at Tebourba was beset by infantry and tanks, its positions penetrated and finally cut off, although, except for the 2d Hampshires, the brigade managed to extricate itself and retire to new positions during the night.

On the 4th, General Eisenhower reported to the CCS that his forces imperatively needed a rest before resuming the march on Tunis.[50] No reserves stood behind the front-line troops, and the air commanders estimated that their squadrons would face a complete breakdown if operations continued as long as a week on the current scale--a scale still not sufficient to support an advance. Existing airdromes were practically bereft of all manner of supplies; maintenance troops, warning service, and AA had to be brought forward to them. More advanced fields had to be occupied and similarly stocked.

In his report the Commander in Chief set a probable target date of 9 December for the resumption of the advance. In the interim, British reinforcements would have come up, some thought would have been given to straightening out the congested railroads east of Constantine, and supplies have been moved forward with the help of the French and their trucks. It was hoped that one or two forward landing strips could be procured for the fighters.

For the Twelfth and the EAC, the breathing-spell recommended in General Eisenhower's report of the 4th would mean the curtailing of fighter activities to occasional sorties against enemy airfields. Bombing, however, would continue unabated (with a new priority--no longer airfields, but ports and LOC) to combat the Axis build-up. To forward this endeavor the theater commander indicated that he would ask Air Marshal Sir Arthur Tedder for heavy bombers from the Middle East or else take an American heavy group from the Eighth Air Force.

Success of the projected 9 December assault depended, of course, on the weather, as protracted rain would make forward airfields unusable, except those at Bone and Maison Blanche, besides facilitating Axis reinforcement. General Eisenhower, who months before had been in favor of abandoning the Casablanca landing to put more strength into Algeria, was finding his pre-invasion fears realized. Not only were his forces insufficient for the task of clearing Tunisia, but the Axis build-up exceeded his own. The Combined Chiefs of Staff approved his plans and stressed a vigorous assault to deprive the Axis of the Tunisian base, so that the Allied forces could be free to take increased precautions to guard the mouth of the Mediterranean.[51]

In accordance with the new policy of restricting the enemy build-up, on 3 December the B-17's attacked the Bizerte docks. At 1043 hours 18 of the 97th Group with 16 P-38's of the 1st Group were over the target at 20,000 feet. The bombers dropped 180 x 500-lb. bombs, scoring hits on two vessels in the canal leading to the harbor, on the canal itself, and on the docks. The heavy flak was more intense than that previously experienced, but the bombers all came through. Radar almost certainly had been installed in the area as the Me-109's were up and waiting. The P-38's were cruising at 25,000 when one of their number fell behind; he was immediately jumped from above by six Me-109's and shot down. Three of his comrades then turned back only to be surprised by a second group of Me-109's. In the ensuing engagement two P-38's were shot down, two listed as missing, and three of the Messerschmitts destroyed.

German defenses were fast being strengthened. Of four P-38's strafing Gabes airdrome on the 3d, intense light flak brought one down and damaged another. Two sweeps over the Tunis area on the 3d both resulted in air battles--in the morning a dozen P-38's engaged 12 Me-109's and 2 FW-190's, reported 1 Lightning missing as against 1 Me-109 destroyed and 2 damaged. In the afternoon, 16 P-38's met 7 Me-109's and 1 FW-190; after a 20-minute fight one P-38 was listed as missing and another crash-landed. The reliable DB-7's also went out-- to El Aouina--9 of them with 12 P-33's escorting. Clouds at 6,000 feet prevented observation of results.[52]

On 4 December, ground activity at the front was restricted to patrolling by both sides, but the Allied forces were counting the damage of the preceding day's battle. The troops were tired and the continual aerial onslaught by German dive bombers did nothing to cheer them. Moreover, until the bombing threat had been lessened, the Allied air could get no rest. In the morning the 301st hammered the Bizerte docks with 150 x 500-pounders, with results described as excellent. A half-hour later, seven B-26's came in on the same target, escorted by eight

P-38's. Bombing from only 4,000 feet, they scored hits on a ship, a warehouse, a railroad station, and oil tanks. One Marauder was lost to the intense light and heavy flak. Eight to 10 Messerschmitts and Focke-Wulfs attacked the escort--which shot down one Me-109 and damaged another. Only five of the eight P-38's returned to Maison Blanche, but two turned up at Bougie and the last at Bone. On that day Bone had sent 16 Spitfires on a sweep, 12 of them belonging to the U. S. 52d Group. Near Tebourba they encountered three Ju-88's accompanied by numerous Me-109's and FW-190's. Although one Me-109 was destroyed, two Spitfires did not return and another crashed in landing.[53]

On 5 December the RAF attempted to use the advanced base at Medjez-el-Bab, but two planes were shot down while landing from a sortie. Next day, the front erupted again, the Germans attacking from El Bathan and Massicault. Again the Allied lines were pierced but the dive bombing had somewhat diminished.

On the 5th the Twelfth Air Force had dispatched its heavies against Tunis harbor and its medium and light bombers against Sidi Ahmed. Sixteen of the 97th's Fortresses blasted the former target from 22,000 feet all of the 150 x 500-lb. load falling on the target area. Docks, sheds, railroad yards, and a merchant vessel sustained hits. On the return, the clouds of smoke from Tunis could be seen at a distance of 50 miles. Only light inaccurate flak was encountered and the dozen escorting P-38's saw no enemy aircraft. Sidi Ahmed took its pounding at midday. First to appear, at 1125, were eight B-25's of the 310th

Group which dropped 56 x 300-pounders on the hangar and among parked aircraft, the six escorting P-38's driving off four enemy fighters which attempted to attack the bombers. One B-25 was missing, believed to have crash-landed 30 miles west of the target. Next came DB-7's with two squadrons of P-38's, one close in, the other on high patrol, but the bombs fell short. As the formations were heading back for Youks, 10 to 15 German fighters appeared and were engaged by six P-38's. One Lightning was shot down and four were reported missing.[54]

By 7 December, ground fighting had definitely subsided; the enemy's attacks decreased in intensity. On 8 December, General Eisenhower approved General Anderson's proposal to withdraw to more defensible ground where the troops could be refitted and built up for another effort. In the midst of the withdrawal, the rains arrived with a vengeance--already on the 7th the weather had begun to hamper air operations and on the next three days it forbade them. Except for the roads and tracks, the terrain became impassible for truck and tank. A major disaster overtook Combat Command B. It became mired during the withdrawal, lost all but three of its eighteen 105-mm. howitzers, all but a dozen of 62 medium tanks and all save 38 out of 122 light tanks. By 11 December, however, General Anderson's forces had retired to the general line Djebel Abiod - Medjez-el-Bab, ensuring the use of the road leading north from Beja and protecting the communications center of Medjez.

In point of fact, the Allies were stuck in Tunisia. General Eisenhower still hoped to mount an offensive which would take Tunis and crowd the enemy into the Bizerte area, but rain was to prevent the carrying out of his plans. He already had settled down to what he had desperately tried to avoid—a "logistic marathon." The Twelfth Air Force, with the other Allied arms, now had to make North Africa more habitable for itself if the area was to become uninhabitable for the Axis.[55]

Chapter III
IMPASSE AND REORGANIZATION

The Anatomy of the Repulse

By 14 December 1942, the Axis establishment in Tunisia numbered an estimated 38,500 men--nearly 20,000 German combat troops and over 11,000 Italian, together with 2,500 GAF and 5,000 service troops. Substantial increments were arriving daily. By the 18th the estimated total had risen to 42,100. Not only were these troops well supplied but an abundance of extra supplies was going down by rail to Sfax and thence by rail, road, and sea to the Afrika Korps in Tripolitania.

In the north Von Arnim was defending his bridgehead along a line west of Mateur-Tebourba-Mohamedia with local attacks employing armor and infantry. With patrols and defensive positions west of Zaghouan and Kairouan, he protected the coastal corridor to the south. Defense of central and southern Tunisia was an affair of outposts and motorized cavalry at Djebel Krechem and Kebili, approximately 50 miles west of Sfax and Gabes, respectively, and at Medenine and Foum Tatahouine, south of the Mareth Line.[1]

While General Eisenhower struggled to extricate his forces from the mud before Tebourba and Mateur for a blow at Tunis, General Montgomery moved along through Libya with the RAF, ME, and the U. S. Ninth Air Force leap-frogging in his train. On 12 December he cracked the defenses at El Agheila, the point where the efforts of his

predecessors Wavell and Auchinleck had begun to subside, and came on
for the next hurdle at Buerat. As the fleeing Rommel neared Von Arnim,
the Northwest African and Middle East theaters began to merge, especially after General Montgomery's planes neutralized Tripoli, restricting the Afrika Korps supply line to the Tunisian ports.[2]

General Anderson's repulse before Tunis was the more bitter because the Allied drive had so nearly grasped the prize--two kitchen trucks reportedly had missed the army and gone undisturbed into the Tunis suburbs--and because the units involved had not spared themselves in the effort. Any number of factors, or a combination of any number, could have accounted for the hair's-breadth failure. For instance, there was the initial role of the French, who had resisted the Allies at Algiers for a whole day and the Germans at El Aouina not at all. Representative of a considerable body of opinion was Adm. Sir Andrew Browne Cunningham's regret that the "bolder" strategy which contemplated an initial assault in the Tunisian area had not prevailed during the planning days. General Eisenhower expressed somewhat the same sentiment in these words: "This force had only enough 'tail' in initial shipments to capture [the] ports. We gambled that with what we had we could grab Tunisia."[3]

The shoestring upon which the Anglo-American forces operated during their career to Djedeida can be as well revealed by incidents as by cold figures. The correspondent David Rame saw British Spitfires with empty guns "stooging around" over Souk el Arba trying to divert or

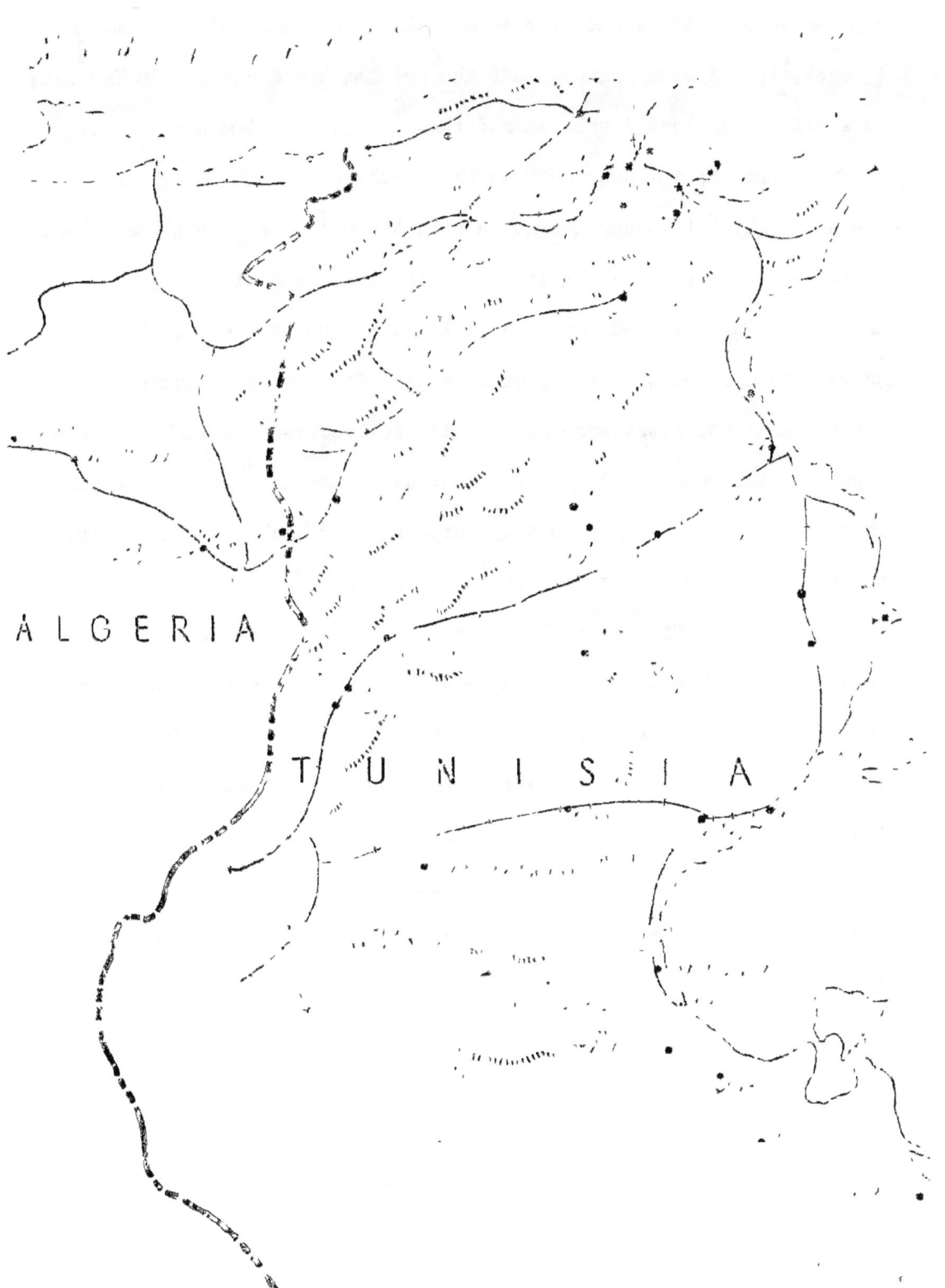

frighten away Me-109's and Ju-87's attacking the town and airdrome. At least, it had been planned that the British would operate in Tunisia; the Americans arrived impromptu and their supplies often started for the front from as far away as Oran or Casablanca. When the ground echelon of the 14th Group caught up with the pilots at Youks they found "a miserable, ragged-looking lot . . . clothes caked with yellow mud. . . . The well-fed look had left their faces." Mess equipment and rations arrived with the ground echelon from Maison Blanche, but no tents and little transportation. The 14th solved the lack of tents by going underground in tarpaulin-covered dugouts and the shortage of transportation by making more trips with fewer vehicles. Such practices were viewed rather as timewasters than hardships.[4]

The ground officers who had lain with their regiments in the hills around Tebourba had their own analyses of failure. They had seen their men dive-bombed continually, had seen this dive bombing perfectly coordinated with tank and infantry attacks, had seen few friendly planes come to the rescue. Reports of harbors bombed evidently did nothing to cheer the foot soldier. Their favorite remedy became the uneconomical--and, in the face of enemy air superiority, ineffective-- air umbrella. Cries of "Stuka" and parallel demands for umbrellas plagued the air commanders. Thenceforth the theory and practice of "air support"--the term currently in use--were much mooted in Northwest Africa.[5]

Although on-the-spot commanders were inclined to censure the RAF and the Twelfth, Generals Eisenhower and Anderson took a more reasonable view of the situation. They realized that the air arm had been as badly overworked as the ground arm, that its airdromes were too few and far away from the front, that its repair, supply, and maintenance facilities were inadequate. Eisenhower summed up the Stuka menace in a cable to the War Department, "Dive bombers have much greater moral than material effect except where we leave an exposed target."

The Commander in Chief called attention to the superiority of Axis troops in the quantity and use of light AA in forward areas. Whereas Allied planes operating at low altitudes were suffering high casualties the inexperienced American troops were not only relatively ill equipped against but also easily demoralized by dive bombing. Consequently, instead of directing a determined fire at the Stuka they could only make determined demands on the air arm for cover. General Eisenhower recommended that defense against dive bombing be given earnest attention in training, and General Marshall so directed.[6]

Not that the air arm made no mistakes of its own. For instance, Rame witnessed an attack by 11 P-38's on an American tank destroyer company near Medjez-el-Bab. The planes made five strafing runs on the bewildered unit, killed five men, and put seven self-propelled guns out of action, despite the fact that identification of the tank destroyers should have been easy as they were the only vehicles in the theater with a large-caliber gun mounted on a half-track.[7]

New Air Bases

Melioration of air support, or of any other aspect of air warfare, waited on the construction and improvement of suitable air bases. A general visiting the theater during December 1942 remarked that all the airdromes presented a perfectly uniform appearance. If the field boasted two hard-surfaced runways, the longer would be employed as a hard-standing and the other, crosswind, for landing. The rest of the landscape was ankle-deep mud. According to report, as many as 285 aircraft were mudbound at Tafaraoui on one night late in November, unable to reach the runways. When some of these planes were later flown to Maison Blanche, congestion was merely shared.[8]

A report of the distribution of Allied aircraft during the first week of December, when the Stukas were braking the advance towards Tunis, illustrates the overcrowding both near the front and at the rear. Excluding French Morocco, the Twelfth and the Eastern Air Command were using 11 fields. Of the three more or less forward airdromes, Bone "housed" 76 fighters, Youks 37 (besides 9 DB-7's), and Souk el Arba 45. Canrobert and Djidjelli some distance behind the front had a total of only 19 fighters and light bombers, but Maison Blanche and Blida in the Algiers area together counted 150 aircraft, and four airdromes around Oran had 180, and it is probable that Maison Blanche and Tafaraoui took the greater part of these concentrations.[9]

In accordance with the over-all TORCH design, the pre-invasion plans for airdrome provision and maintenance accepted a territorial division of responsibility between British and Americans, the British initially assuming responsibility for the Eastern Task Force Area. With the linking of the Center and Eastern Task Forces, the American area was to be pushed eastward as fast as Twelfth Air Force engineer units could take over. In addition the Twelfth Air Force contingent carried the burden in the Center and Western Task Force areas--Western Algeria and Morocco.

Into Oran from England, the Twelfth Air Force brought four battalions of aviation engineers, the 809th, 814th, 815th and 817th, considered the best prepared units of this kind in the United Kingdom. Attached to XII Air Support Command were the 21st Aviation Engineer Regiment, less three battalions, and two companies of the 871st Airborne Engineer Battalion, Aviation. The latter unit had been activated at Westover Field on 18 August 1942 and only the utmost dispatch got the two companies readied for TORCH. The Twelfth's aviation engineers were more numerous, better staffed and equipped, than their British counterparts--who were actually army troops attached to an army, as opposed to an air force, headquarters--and they proved more efficient in the use and understanding of heavy equipment.[10]

Brig. Gen. Donald A. Davison, theater engineer--Col. John O. Colonna was Twelfth Air Force engineer--characterized the airdrome problem as one of "manpower and mud." The American battalions were forced to divide their attention among several requirements: preparing the major base areas around Casablanca, Oran, and Algiers; supplementing the efforts of the British construction groups forward; providing bases for a Twelfth Air Force operating where it had not been planned to operate so soon; and, in deference to the requirement which constantly vexed TORCH, preparing bases for use in case Spain or Spanish Morocco were involved in a hostile combination. To the very end of the Tunisian campaign a string of border fighter fields was continually stocked against this last-mentioned eventuality--Meknes, Ras El Ma, Fez, Taza, and Guercif; and a half-dozen bomber fields were readied in the Oran-Mascara region.[11]

As for the mud, it was practically universal that winter. The British, who maintained from the time of the landings two airdrome construction groups, found a particularly stubborn variety in the Medjerda valley, the natural highway to Tunis. Detachments of their 14th Airfield Construction Group, initially engaged at Maison Blanche and Blida, moved forward to Djidjelli, Setif, Philippeville, and Bone, and by 20 November were in the area of Souk el Arba. When the rains came at Souk el Arba, Sommerfeld mat simply sank in the mud; when an underlayer of cork was added, it buckled and the Spits proceeded to rip up large chunks of the runway. No better success was had with bamboo rushes. The answer to the Medjerda valley mud grew out of a resident Frenchman's remark that he had a field which never became waterlogged. Its soil was sandy. Thus the new British airdromes were built on a number of sand outcrops in the Souk el Khemis area.[12]

After the GAF's raids on Maison Blanche in mid-November, the Twelfth went on a hunt for airdromes--dry airdromes and airdromes for dispersal. Up in the Algerian plateau the climate was known to be somewhat drier than in the coastal area, and at Telergma, in the Rhumel valley 20 miles southeast of Constantine, a very small field was discovered. Arabs, French troops, and aviation engineers worked on the site from 2 to 7 December and on the latter date it was ready for Twelfth Air Force mediums. The 310th Group (B-25's) and the 319th (B-26's) were scheduled to come in from Maison Blanche on the 13th and B-26's of the 17th Group on either the 14th or 15th.[13]

A base for the mediums had been achieved, but General Doolittle was anxious to move his B-17's out of Tafaraoui to an all-weather airdrome. For this, the Rhumel valley was too wet, and recourse was had to the desert itself, at Biskra. An oasis and winter resort, Biskra lay beyond the Atlas mountains, about 120 miles south of the Mediterranean and connected with it by a railroad from Philippeville. It possessed a field that could be enlarged, and the airborne engineers then working in Morocco undertook the task. Fifty-six C-47's flew the men and their equipment to Biskra. On 13 December, twenty-four hours after their arrival, the first B-17's came in on the expanded field. Biskra's climate could be expected to be favorable during the winter months, but mid-March would bring a south wind off the Sahara and sand storms would make operations impossible. Therefore, it was planned to move the B-17's to Telergma by that date. Actually they moved earlier.[14]

At Biskra, in December and January, logistical operations were of the simplest. A daily 250 tons had been allotted to the base on the railroad from Philippeville--one train a day with gas, food, and bombs. Here again the C-47's were lifesavers. It was reported that when the

B-17's took off for the Tunisian docks, they frequently took with them all the bombs the field possessed, and no more were available until the C-47's came in that day with pay load for another strike. On 4 January General Cannon, by then CG, XII Bomber Command, stated that he had to reduce operations lest his units run out of 500-pounders altogether.[15]

Down in the southern sector, by the first week in December, XII Fighter Command was operating P-40's of the 33d Group out of Thelepte, 40 miles southeast of Tebessa, near the site of an ancient Roman city. Gafsa, even farther to the south and east, offered a potential air base site, but the Allies' hold on the surrounding countryside was too precarious to permit its utilization. In December one of the airborne engineer companies was flown in to work at Youks and Thelepte and at Tebessa itself, where an inoperational airdrome was reported on 1 January.[16]

Despite the undisputed skill of the American aviation engineers, the progress of airdromes was impeded by factors for which no immediate remedy was at hand at Twelfth Air Force headquarters. The battalions had been stinted on equipment in the initial allotments and, to make matters worse, outside Oran a submarine put a torpedo into a ship loaded with bulldozers and other machinery. The Twelfth vigorously pressed Washington for its replacement and for special heavy equipment as well, and by January 1943 some was on the way. The rainy Tunisian winter made all-weather airdromes almost a necessity and a sufficiency of steel plank and Sommerfeld track had been provided in the convoys. But the weight of these materials taxed the already war-weary African railroads. To surface one runway required 2,000 tons of steel matting, which absorbed the capacity of the railroad in the forward area for an entire day.[17]

On 1 January 1943, General Spaatz, by then serving as General Eisenhower's principal air adviser, cabled the COS his short-term program for North African airdrome development, which, incidentally was drawn with a backward glance at the Strait of Gibraltar. Facing Tunisia he envisioned two dry-weather heavy-bomber fields in the Telergma area, to be ready by 5 January, and four all-weather medium-bomber bases in the Canrobert-Ain Beida area, to be completed by 1 March. Ten fighter fields had already been located, but additional all-weather fields would be constructed at Gafsa, Maknassy, and Sbeitla, all forward of Thelepte. This latter construction presupposed an Allied advance in the southern sector, for which plans were actually underway by New Year's Day 1943. First, however, General Anderson was to have another unsuccessful try at the Medjerda route.[18]

Bomber Reinforcements

Despite the discouraging situation on the northern sector, General Eisenhower still sought after decisive action to break the deadlock. He decided on an attack about 20 December with Tunis as the minimum objective. After the mudding down of Combat Command B, primacy of armor in such a stroke was impossible. Accordingly, it was planned that the Allies' air power would be exploited to the utmost and their vastly superior artillery employed to smash the enemy tanks. On 16 December, Generals Eisenhower and Anderson were exchanging messages regarding the switching of the "strategic" bombing effort to targets in the path of the First Army. On the previous day, General Anderson had sent in an appreciation of his build-up for a D-day of 22 December. The build-up was none too impressive; it could be disrupted by any large-scale fighting before the target date, or by any slow-up along the LOC. After seven days of hard fighting, his units would be short of ammunition and could not be withdrawn for refitting.

Renewed rain effectively frustrated the plan. Off the roads, no vehicle could be maneuvered; the Commander in Chief saw four men vainly trying to extricate a motorcycle which had mired in a grassy field. At the airfields broken stone sank in the mud, and for a period after 18 December operations virtually closed down. Without air power and the maneuver of artillery no blow against Tunis could succeed. Bitterly disappointed, General Eisenhower finally called off the attack on the day before Christmas, after it had been twice postponed.[19]

In the absence of a land push requiring an effort against tactical objectives, the primary targets of the Twelfth's heavy bombers remained Tunis and Bizerte, with occasional excursions against Sfax and Sousse. As the main factor in the continued German-Italian build-up, these ports became the preoccupation of all Allied aircraft which profitably could be brought to bear against them. The Ninth Air Force had hit at the major onloading port of Naples on 4 December and on the 15th its B-24's struck Sfax, opening on the Tunisian depots an assault which soon reached north to Tunis itself. Malta, by now an important offensive base, had been assigned Wellingtons in November to aid the TORCH project, and concentrated its effort chiefly on the port of Sousse. During November and December, Malta-based aircraft dropped 644 (British) tons of bombs on Tunisian targets.[20]

On 3 December, General Eisenhower, considering the bomber force available against Tunis and Bizerte insufficient to combat Axis reinforcement, signified his intention of seeking its augmentation from the United Kingdom or the Middle East. Air Marshal Welsh therefore requested two Wellington squadrons from the Air Ministry. The British Chiefs of Staff, reasoning that help could come more quickly from the Middle East, asked Air Marshal Tedder to lend the squadrons, but the latter felt that the force could not be spared and suggested that RAF Bomber Command be called upon. General Eisenhower joined him in this sentiment, and 142 and 150 Squadrons, armed with Wellington III's, went down to Portreath on 9 December for staging, the first aircraft landing at Blida on 19 December. Rains kept them inactive for over a week but on the night of 28-29 December they went out after the Bizerte docks. Together with the Eastern Air Command's 326 Wing (Bisleys and Hurribombers), which moved forward from Blida to Setif and Canrobert in early December, the Wellingtons nightly supplemented XII Bomber Command's missions.[21]

The Eighth Air Force was also drawn upon. On 5 December Maj. Gen. Ira C. Eaker ordered the air echelon of three squadrons of the 93d Group (B-24's) to move to Africa as soon as possible. On 7 December these aircraft arrived at Tafaraoui from Portreath and Exeter. This Oran base was described as "unfit for operations because of short runways, lack of hard-standings, the wet field, inadequate service and maintenance, as well as poor housing and messing." Three planned missions were called off on account of rain, and a fourth on 12 December was canceled when one of the first ships to start taxiing collapsed a nose wheel in the mud. On the 13th, however, Bizerte was attacked.[32]

Nineteen of the Liberators left at 0845 on the long flight. Over Bizerte at 1205 hours at altitudes from 20,500 to 21,000 feet, they dropped 74 x 1,000-lb. bombs, scoring hits on the docks, amid intense and accurate flak. One element was attacked from above by three Me-109's followed by another coming in from the front. With an engine damaged, one B-24 dropped behind and was badly shot up, crash-landing near Maison Blanche. On the following day, the 93d ran its second and last mission from Algeria when 12 B-24's returned to Bizerte, dropped 60 x 1,000-lb. bombs, straddling a ship in the harbor and hitting the docks. A dozen blue-green, camouflaged Me-109's intercepted, employing a new tactic. Three approached a B-24 from five miles out; when close in, one swung right as a diversion, the other broke left and attacked off beam and to the side; the single Messerschmitt then came in on the other side. Despite this novelty, three Me-109's were shot down and the B-24's returned unscathed.

After this brief stay in Tafaraoui's mud, the 93d departed for the Middle East. It flew out on 15 December and landed at LG 139, Gambut Main, Cyrenaica, coming under the control of IX Bomber Command. For a time the 93d found no better weather in the Western Desert, but after Christmas it began hitting the Tunisian ports from the east. The transfer of the 93d's three squadrons was a result of an agreement with the Ninth Air Force, by which the 513th Squadron (B-17's) was shifted to Northwest Africa. The 93d could be better employed in the Middle East whence the B-24's superior range enabled strikes at Naples and Palermo. The B-17's, on the other hand, could be profitably used against Tunis and Bizerte from the Algerian bases. By the terms of the agreement, the 93d's overriding targets were those affecting the campaign to clear Tunisia.[23]

The Assault on the Ports

Available records are silent on many details of XII Bomber Command's early career in North Africa. The organization had arrived in the theater under the command of Col. Claude E. Duncan, but on or about 24 November General Eisenhower was requesting that Col. Charles T. Phillips from the Eighth Air Force's 3d Wing be flown to Africa as a replacement. Colonel Phillips' command was of short duration: he took over around 11 December and on the 15th was killed on a B-26 mission over El Aouina. Headquarters had been successively moved from Tafaraoui to Algiers to Constantine, and Col. Carlyle H. Ridenour, CO of the Constantine echelon, assumed command on 16 December. On New Year's Day General Cannon was brought over from XII Air Support Command, and he continued in charge of XII Bomber Command until the activation of Northwest African Air Forces on 18 February.[24]

If details of its activities remain vague, XII Bomber Command's mission during this period was clear enough. On 31 December General Doolittle cabled Bomber Command headquarters at Constantine as follows: "Until further notice your mission is to destroy docks, shipping, and marshalling yards at Tunis and Bizerte, using maximum force consistent with a sustained effort. . . ." That a similar directive was in force prior to that time is scarcely to be doubted. From 12 December to the end of the month XII Bomber Command's heavies ran five missions against Tunis, seven against Bizerte, and three apiece against Sfax and Sousse. It is probable that the last raids were undertaken on occasions when weather forbade forays against the northern ports. From 1 to 8 January seven missions were flown, six of them to Tunis and Bizerte and their satellite harbors of La Goulette and Ferryville.[25]

Daylight pounding of the major ports was by now strictly a task for heavy bombers. With the continued build-up of the Axis bridgehead, the area of Tunis and Bizerte became too hot for medium or light bombers, more vulnerable alike to light flak and to enemy fighters, even when escorted. No longer as in the first days of December could the DB-7's go to El Aouina or the mediums to the Bizerte docks, although occasionally the mediums attacked difficult targets when B-17's were along to saturate the defenses.[26]

B-17 accuracy proved generally excellent. On 12 December, 17 aircraft of the 301st Group placed all but six out of 100 bombs on the docks and marshalling yards at Tunis, leaving fires in the area and a ship with a bomb hole on one side. On the 13th, a contingent from the 97th Group hit and probably sank another vessel at the Tunis docks. The 301st performed a successful mission on the 13th, destroying a ship at Bizerte and causing large fires on the docks. Next day, the 97th came back to shower the same target with 42½ tons of high explosive.[27]

As operations go, the early missions had been rather easy. On 30 November, General Doolittle reported that since D-day only eight Twelfth Air Force aircraft were shot down by enemy planes and 12 by ground fire, friendly or hostile. Seven had been lost on the ground by enemy bombing and strafing and 49 through miscellaneous and unknown causes. The last "rather appalling" figure comprised not only losses due to crashes, disappearances and internments but also aircraft temporarily out of commission. Personnel losses were comparatively slight; pilots often walked home from crashes and the Arabs received considerable blood money. However, after their fields recovered from the rainy spell which began on 8 December, the Allied airmen found that the Germans had employed the interval to strengthen defenses. The B-17's discovered new and formidable yellow-nosed FW-190's at Bizerte and flak on a marked increase.[28]

On 15 December the 301st, from its new home at Biskra, was attacking the Tunis docks and marshalling yards with 49 x 500-pounders. The Germans raised a smoke screen which made observation of results difficult and sent up intense heavy flak and 25 FW-190's and Me-109's to the defense. Notwithstanding, the seven B-17's and six escorting P-38's landed safely at base, preliminary estimates showing six enemy aircraft destroyed. Simultaneously, 12 more of the 301st's aircraft, with a half-dozen more of the 1st Fighter Group's P-38's, bombed Bizerte, obtaining good results and fighting off six enemy fighters.[29]

On the 17th, both heavy bomb groups were again active. The 301st attacked the docks at Tunis and La Goulette, dropping 55 x 1,000-lb. bombs on the former and 30 x 1,000-pounders on the latter target and scoring a direct hit on a ship at Tunis. Sixteen of the 97th's B-17's smashed at Bizerte, both missions reporting intense and accurate heavy flak. On the next day, the 97th and 301st contributed 18 Forts each to a raid on Bizerte harbor. Opposition was heavy, 15 enemy fighters attacking for as many minutes after the bombers left the target. As a result, four of 16 escorting P-38's of the 1st Group were lost in combat, one B-17 shot down, and another forced to crash-land at Le Kef. Thirty-three B-17's had bombed the target; the remaining three Forts dropped on two naval vessels off Bizerte between Cape Zebib and the Cani Islands and scored a direct hit on a light cruiser, setting it afire.[30]

Thereafter, until 26 December, foul weather plagued the bombers. On the 21st at Sfax and Gabes and on the 22d at Bizerte, Sousse, and Sfax, 10/10 cloud foiled the attack. On the 23d, 17 B-17's of the 301st, escorted by 11 P-38's of the 1st Group, took off in an attempt to bomb the airdromes at Tunis and Bizerte. Five bombers returned early as a result of cumulus and icing at 25,000; the target had been completely shrouded. Four aircraft did not return to base, but turned up at distant Tafaraoui, Nouvion, and Relizane.[31]

By the end of December XII Bomber Command organization began to take form, incorporating one new principle which usually has been traced back to the Northwest African Air Forces. The principle was the attachment of escort fighters to the bomber command. Between 14 and 18 December, two squadrons of the 1st Fighter Group moved from Youks and Maison Blanche to the bomber station at Biskra. It is probable that they at once came under the control of XII Bomber Command.[32] Placing escort fighters under the bomber commander did away with the necessity of coordinating each mission with XII Fighter Command and simplified such problems as rendezvous. With the poor communications then obtaining in Africa---General Doolittle on 30 November rated communications as the chief bugbear of efficient operations---any diminution of channels was a blessing. The appearance of the P-38's under the Bomber Command may also have derived from General Doolittle's plans for breaking the African area into districts, each controlled by a composite wing operating both bombers and fighters.[33]

In the early days, XII Bomber Command passed down directly to the groups operational instructions for the missions chosen by higher echelons. However, as the available groups became more numerous, wings were interposed. For this purpose the headquarters units of the 5th Bomb Wing and the 7th Fighter Wing, originally attached to XII Air Support Command, were utilized. On Christmas Day, Colonel Atkinson, CO of the 97th Group, was promoted to brigadier general and later made CG of the 5th Bomb Wing (Heavy), this wing gradually assembling at Biskra in mid-January. Shortly after New Year's, personnel of the 7th Fighter Wing Headquarters were alerted for a move from Morocco, and on 7 January Colonel Ridenour replaced Col. John C. Crosthwaite as commanding officer. On 1 February the 7th began operating at Chateaudun du Rhumel, near Constantine, as a medium bombardment wing, an arrangement formalized when it was redesignated 47th Bomb Wing (Medium) on 25 February.[34]

After Christmas, the spell of bad weather having worn off, the heavy bombers returned to their offensive against the Tunisian ports. On 26 December the 97th went to Bizerte, encountering what was described as a "solid wall" of heavy flak which exploded one B-17 over the target and forced another to crash-land near Souk el Arba. Two of eight escorting P-38's were lost during the mission and three FW-190's were assessed as destroyed. On the same day, the 301st went to Sfax, escorted by P-40's of the 33d Group. The bombers wrought havoc in the port, claiming one small and two large vessels sunk. The flak was slight and no enemy aircraft appeared.[35]

The southern ports were gaining in importance at this period as supplies were built up there on anticipation of Rommel's arrival in Tunisia, and three missions apiece were run against Sfax and Sousse in five days. Notably, on 27 December, 14 B-17's of the 301st blasted Sousse with 66 x 1,000-lb. and 30 x 500-lb. bombs. Direct hits were claimed on four ships, one of which was blown to bits, and docks and warehouses were severely damaged. No enemy aircraft challenged any of these missions, and the flak was not formidable. Weather prevented observation of the results of the strike at Sousse on the 29th. Sfax took its turn on the last two days of the month. The 97th started fires in the marshalling yards and on the west end of the North Quay on the 30th, and the 301st scored hits on two medium-sized ships in the harbor on the 31st.[36]

The 97th Group observed New Year's Day with a highly successful blow at Tunis harbor, 17 B-17's obtaining hits on the docks and the whole of the target area including the electric railroad yard. No enemy aircraft were seen and all aircraft got safely home. But on the 2d the Axis defenses erupted against the 301st. Twenty B-17's and eight P-38's arrived over La Goulette shortly after noon. The bombers dropped 223 x 500-lb. bombs at an altitude of from 21,500 to 23,500 feet, scoring on an ore-loading depot, a camp, a shipyard and dry docks, and the powerhouse. Two merchant vessels were hit, and one probably was sunk. Enemy reaction was well conceived. Just before the AA ceased, white bursts were seen, evidently a signal to the fighters (Me-109's and Italian), 40 to 50 of which promptly attacked the bombers. Simultaneously a dozen yellow-nosed Me-109's engaged the P-38's cruising at 26,000 feet. Two P-38's were shot down as against two Me-109's destroyed, two probably destroyed and two damaged. All the B-17's got back to base, one badly flak-damaged, and the bombers claimed 14 enemy fighters destroyed, 8 probables, and 13 damaged.

On 3 January Biskra underwent the second of a series of Axis bombing attacks when six Ju-88's attacked the field at dusk, just after the airdrome fighter patrol had landed, their bombs damaging several B-17's. On the previous day a lone Ju-88 had come out of the clouds from the south and dumped its load harmlessly short of the target. These events accelerated the progress of fox-holes and dugouts, the Bomber Command personnel going underground in much the same manner as the units out at Youks had done. Moreover, probably as a result of the raid of the 3d, the 2d Squadron of the 52d Group, veteran of many battles over Bone, was ordered to Biskra for airdrome patrol, the 52d's 4th Squadron replacing it at the Algerian port. By now all echelons of the 1st Fighter Group were operating from Biskra, group headquarters and the 27th Squadron having arrived on 26, 28, and 30 December by C-47, truck convoy, and rail.[37]

On 4 January both Bizerte and Tunis were cloud-covered and only one B-17 was able to drop its load of 500-pounders on La Goulette. However, on the 5th and the 8th, the B-17's demonstrated what their bombsights could do. The 5th saw the 97th Group over Sfax, weather reconnaissance having disclosed solid overcast at the more northerly ports. Seven B-17's returned early, but the remaining 11 bombed the Sfax power station. The station was assessed as completely destroyed and the escorting P-38's reported that their charges had hit, in addition, two vessels in the harbor and left the entire dock area in flames. Bad weather did not protect Ferryville on the 8th. Twenty-six P-38's furnished escort, destroyed one Me-109 and one FW-190, and drove off 15 to 20 enemy fighters south of Porto Farina. Sixteen B-17's of the 301st Group bombed the naval base at Bizerte through holes in the overcast but results were not observed. Fifteen of the 97th's Forts, however, finding similar holes over Ferryville, released 84 x 500-lb. and 18 x 1,000-lb. bombs from 23,500. Of 15 to 20 enemy fighters intercepting, they shot down one Me-109 and one FW-190, and probably three others, and reported hits on oil storage tanks, docks, and ships. Not until Tunis had fallen in May were known the full results of that day's work at Ferryville: sunk or damaged beyond repair, the French submarine Nautilus, the sailing vessel Gascogne, the tug Cyclone, the aircraft tender Petrel, and the patrol vessel Ypres.[38]

The Mediums

During the period from 12 December to 8 January, the excellent German flak began definitely to limit the employment of the mediums, driving them to greater bombing altitudes and less well-defended targets.

On-the-deck approaches were also abandoned, not only because of intense light AA fire over the battle lines, but because clouds of birds flew up from the Tunisian olive groves, smashing the plexiglas in the nose and upper turrets and inflicting scalp wounds on the crew members.[39]

Although a number of unsuccessful forays were made against shipping at sea, targets were primarily airdromes, marshalling yards, and railroad bridges. Sousse harbor was twice attacked, but the ports otherwise remaining the special province of the heavies. Initially, most of these B-25 and B-26 missions were on an extremely modest scale. For a period after 5 December the 310th's striking power consisted of a half-dozen B-25's, and the heaviest attack prior to the new year was mounted by 13 medium bombers--the combined resources of the 310th and the 319th. The latter organization continued to lose its commanding officers: Lt. Col. Sam. W. Agee had succeeded Major Jones but both were shot down and made prisoners while participating in a raid on Bizerte on 4 December.[40]

The first attempt by mediums to bomb Sousse harbor was frustrated on 12 December by wintry weather in which two B-26's were lost, but on the two succeeding days successful strikes were accomplished. On the 13th, the 310th's B-25's went over at 7,000 to 7,800 feet, six of them with four escorting P-38's. They hit the storage sheds ringing the port, one ship at the docks, and another large one in the harbor. On the return, one B-25 with an engine out dropped behind and headed north 50 miles from the target. Next day, the Sousse antiaircraft gunners were apparently caught by surprise when six of the 319th's B-26's swept in at 900 to 1,200 feet, hit the docks and three vessels in the harbor, and, with their P-38 escort, got away unscathed.[41]

The demise of this particular tactic, however, came quickly. At El Aouina on the 15th, seven B-26's came in at from 600 to 1,000 feet and bombed successfully, claiming six to 10 enemy planes destroyed on the ground. Intense light and heavy flak was encountered, to which, south of Carthage, four destroyers and a cruiser also contributed. As a result one flak-hit Marauder plunged into the Gulf of Tunis. Low-level bombing signally failed to confuse the AA on 18 December when four P-38's of the 1st Group escorted five B-26's and six B-25's to the Sousse marshalling yards. Bombing was from 700 to 1,500 feet and the 300-pounders fell on the station and roundhouse, on a freight train, and on 2,000 feet of track. A mile-long box barrage greeted the formation and two B-26's were lost, one with an engine out defiantly continuing to fire at the flak barges until it crashed into the harbor. After this reception, low-level bombing was virtually abandoned, except against targets where little or no AA was indicated.[42]

After the Sousse mission on the 18th, no medium bomber operations seem to have taken place for over 10 days. The interval was probably spent sweating out bad weather and practicing minimum-altitude bombing, soon to be effectively employed against shipping in the Sicilian narrows. When operations were resumed on 30 December, the bombing effort was concentrated on airdromes—the mediums having largely taken over this counter-air force function from the heavies—and on the Tunisian railroad complex which by now carried most of the supplies for Rommel as well as for the growing Axis establishment in central and southern Tunisia.[43] On the first day, a fresh B-26 unit made its debut when six Marauders from the 17th Bomb Group hit the Gabes airdrome, while the 310th was dropping on the marshalling yards at Sfax. The 17th's air echelon had arrived over the southern route via Natal, Accra, and Bathurst. On the 31st it paid the Gabes field a return visit with a dozen B-26's, escorted by 10 P-40's of the 33d Fighter Group. They dropped 200 x 100-lb. demolition bombs and 20 x 100-lb. frags, the first time fragmentation bombs are mentioned in operations in Africa. Two enemy fighters attacked the B-26's, downing one which had first been hit by flak.[44]

On New Year's Day, while the 310th was moving to Berteaux, another of the fields being developed in the Constantine area, the 17th, escorted by P-40's, went to the stoutly defended Tunis marshalling yards where intense and accurate light and heavy flak accounted for one out of nine B-26's, and the P-40's lost one of their number in an argument with a half-dozen Me-109's. On the 4th, 18 B-26's of the 310th fought 4/10 to 10/10 cloud to drop HE and incendiaries on the Kairouan railroad yards.[45] The same day saw the 17th involved in an unusual encounter. Eleven of its B-26's had taken off at 1255 for a rendezvous over Feriana with P-40's based at near-by Thelepte. On arriving over the town the pilots saw the Thelepte airdrome under attack by five Ju-88's, escorted by as many Me-109's, and turned their aircraft for home. The escorting Messerschmitts at once engaged the American bombers--to their cost, for the B-26's promptly destroyed two of the attackers while suffering only minor damage to one of their own number.

Besides discovering that unescorted B-26's were not to be lightly assaulted, the German force sustained additional losses when Thelepte's P-40's made interception. The Ju-88's came in low along a road to the northeast of the airdrome, pulled up into the clouds, and one after the other dive-bombed across the field. One P-40 was destroyed on the ground, but five others took off, shot down one Ju-88 and one of the remaining Me-109's. The Air Intelligence Report incidentally described the raid as being led by a four-engined aircraft, probably navigating for the Ju-88's.[46]

From 5 to 8 January the holy city of Kairouan came in for a share of the mediums' attention. On the 5th, P-38's of the newly operational 82d Group escorted B-26's of the 17th on a frag attack on the airdrome, a performance repeated three days later, and on the 6th the 310th hit hard at the town's railroad yards. On the 7th, the 17th went down to Gabes, to attack the airdrome and adjacent barracks with a mixture of frag, HE, and incendiaries.[47]

During this period, the mediums made three full-dress attacks, two of them successful, on vital railroad bridges. On 13 December, the 319th sent eight B-26's escorted by four P-38's against a bridge three miles north of La Hencha, on the coast railroad between Sousse and Sfax. Five B-26's attacked from 1,000 to 2,000 feet with 42 x 300-lb. bombs, destroying the bridge with two direct hits on the center span. On 2 January a dozen B-26's of the 17th Group with P-40 escort struck unsuccessfully at a structure five miles north of El Djem, but the 310th had better fortune six days later. First target, in the morning, was a junction at Kalaa Srira, just west of Sousse, where a branch line ran east to Kairouan. The six B-25's went on to tear up 100 yards of roadbed near Ben Zina, 12 miles southwest of Kairouan. In the afternoon, Graiba, a three-way junction 35 miles southwest of Sfax, was attacked. Of the three bridges at Graiba, two were reported totally destroyed and the third severely damaged by a 66 x 500-lb. load dropped from 2,000 feet by a dozen Mitchells. However, such infrequent attacks could not seriously interrupt the Axis build-up.[48]

XII Fighter Command

Until relieved in the southern sector by XII Air Support Command early in January, XII Fighter Command maintained two headquarters, one at La Senia airdrome at Oran, the other about 500 airline miles away at Tebessa. The Oran headquarters, which on 16 December became known as the Western Algerian Composite Wing, evidently concerned itself with the administration and training of Air Corps units in the area and with air defense, convoy protection, and antisubmarine patrols. Tebessa, on the other hand, became the headquarters of the CO, XII

Fighter Command, Col. Thomas W. Blackburn, who had brought the Command down from England and was promoted to brigadier general on 11 December. General Blackburn had charge of the most advanced American air units in the theater, those based at Youks-les-Bains and Thelepte.[49]

For five to six weeks after their establishment in the Tebessa region XII Fighter Command's aircraft worked mostly under British control. The Youks contingent had been given over to the British 78th Division on 27 November, when the initial Tunis push was at its height—an arrangement somewhat modified on 5 December when AFHQ decreed that 15 sorties might be provided daily for Colonel Raff's local paratroop force as against 25 for the First Army. On the 14th, in preparation for General Anderson's projected renewal of the drive on Tunis, Group Capt. G. M. Lawson, commanding the RAF's 242 Group, received operational direction of all U. S. squadrons in the Tebessa area. Here again, however, exceptions were made for air reconnaissance over Gabes, Gafsa, and Sousse, and for missions adjudged necessary to the security of American and French forces in southern Tunisia. Direct British control probably ceased late in December after the postponement of the First Army offensive. On Christmas Day Air Marshal Welsh suggested that it should, and no missions were flown to the northern sector after 30 December.[50]

The pioneer units, 14th Fighter Group, 15th Light Bombardment Squadron, and the 94th Squadron of the 1st Fighter Group, had learned a good deal by mid-December. The P-38's had sustained considerable losses in the early days when they habitually went up to the Tunis-Bizerte area, six or eight strong escorting a half-dozen DB-7's, matched against the local GAF superiority. They succeeded in protecting the bombers well enough; indeed the 15th's losses were astonishingly light throughout its operations. However, the German pursuit took advantage of the fact that the P-38's were usually short of gas on the return trip and could not afford to stay and fight. As to the relative performance of the rival fighters, the P-38 stacked up well. It could outrun the Me-109 and FW-190 at all altitudes, although this was possible only if the pilot ignored the maximum power limit; and with the use of the combat flaps it would outturn both German types, which often spun attempting to follow. In a climb the Messerschmitt and Focke-Wulf enjoyed only a greater initial surge, but the Lightning could not dive with them, at as steep an angle or with as rapid a pull-out.[51]

The 15th Light Bombardment Squadron, probably due to its operational background in England, seems to have taken the African theater in its stride. Even at Youks it reported good maintenance, the ground crews consisting largely of "old Army men." The pilots flew the DB-7, export version of the A-20, equipped with British bombsights and to carry British bombs.

The 15th flew missions from Youks until the first week in January, when its aircraft and organizational equipment were ordered transferred to the 47th Light Bombardment Group and officers and men were moved back to the Oran area, the pilots eventually returning to the United States in March. Bombing technique was similar to that employed under the Eighth Air Force in that level bombing was the rule, usually from 6,500 to 8,000 feet, below the effective range of the 88-mm. and at the limit of the light Bofors AA. The DB-7's went out at 500 feet to avoid the radar, 10 minutes before the target was reached climbed to 8,000, then, after bombing, dived to the deck for the journey home. Flak often proved so intense and accurate that the formations adopted the expedient of climbing to as high as 11,000 five miles from the target and then performing a shallow dive at 300 mph to bombing altitude, meanwhile employing, as evasive action, course changes of 30 degrees.

Low-level bombing, in the unanimous opinion of the pilots, was inadvisable on several counts. The minimum safe fuze setting, for one thing, was 11 seconds, giving a mobile target time to get out of the way. They stated that not one out of 10 bombs directed at an artillery position would score a hit and that against such targets dive bombing was the answer. Moreover, in low-level operations planes and personnel took an "extreme beating" from light flak.[52]

Operations went on, organization evolved, and new units were sent down to XII Fighter Command at Tebessa. A detachment of the 47th Light Bomb Group was at Youks by 13 December, and elements of the 33d Fighter Group had gone into action on the 7th. As additional fighters came in, the P-38's were withdrawn for escort work at stations farther back. Between 14 and 18 December the 94th Squadron was sent to join the parent 1st Group at Biskra, and the 14th Fighter moved to Berteaux on 9 January to begin work with the B-25's.[53]

Of the new units, the 47th Light Bombardment Group, under Lt. Col. F. R. Terrell, had come to Africa in seven echelons and detachments, some by way of the United Kingdom with the A-20B's, all gradually assembling at Mediouna air base in French Morocco, where for a time they carried on training. Shortly, however, the movement to the front began. Six planes of the 97th Squadron arrived on 13 December at Youks, where until 9 January, when another increment of personnel arrived, there were just six men, excluding the crews, to service them: four mechanics, one armament man, and one radio man. On 28 December, 13 additional A-20's arrived at Thelepte.

In the United States, the 47th had been trained in low-level air support, an expensive form of aerial warfare in Africa. It arrived in the battle area without bombsights or bombardiers and consequently, in the midst of combat operations at Youks and Thelepte, it was necessary to retrain the group to a large extent. Pilots studied evasive action, breakaways, and cooperation with fighter escort; volunteer bombardiers began working at medium-level bombing with the British Mark IX-E sight; and mechanics transferred bomb controls from cockpit to nose. In fact, after the repulse of the Germans and Italians in the battles around Kasserine Pass in February, the 47th was withdrawn to Canrobert for training as well as refitting.[54]

Commanded by Lt. Col. William W. Momyer, the 33d Fighter Group had also come up from Morocco, where it had been assigned to XII Air Support Command. After it had arrived in Africa via the catapults on the U. S. S. Chenango and H. M. S. Archer, its regular squadrons were stationed at Cazes and Craw fields and its advance replacements at Rabat. About its movement to the front, little is known except for the irregular way Maj. Philip Cochran accomplished the transfer.

Major Cochran had commanded the first replacements, known as the "advance attrition," of the 33d--34 pilots and 35 P-40F's--which were catapulted off the Archer on the D plus 5 convoy. At Rabat the replacements had no T/O, no mess, and no medical facilities and subsisted on the generosity of neighboring organizations. Major Cochran christened them the "Joker" squadron and they proceeded to train and fly patrols in the vicinity. Eventually Cochran and seven other pilots were ordered to fly to Oujda, where the P-40's were to be taken from them and sent on to the Tunisian front. The upshot was that Cochran arrived at Thelepte to take command, as ranking officer, of two halves of two squadrons of the 33d which had proceeded to that most forward of all American airdromes.65

Although less subject to miring than Youks, Thelepte was by no stretch of the imagination an ideal operating base. It had no radar and properly speaking no warning net. However, Colonel Raff and his paratroops were at Feriana and the French did what they could to aid, placing gendarmes at Fondouk and Sidi Bou Zid and other points to the east. These latter telephoned in when they observed planes in flight but, unskilled in identification, they reported all aircraft as hostile. In the Sbeitla-Kasserine region there were Deuxieme Bureau operatives, who knew the Arabs right through to Tunis and obtained information on such matters as bomb damage, and even an Alsatian interrogator skilled enough to get technical aircraft information out of prisoners.[56]

So far as Thelepte's antiaircraft defense was concerned, the 47th Group found on its arrival four 40-mm. Bofors and four .50-cal. machine guns. Youks could boast eleven 40-mm., four 90-mm. and a few .50-cal. positions. Day airdrome patrol was maintained over both fields and, although the Ju-88's came in frequently, their bombing was not very effective and they paid heavily to the P-40's and P-38's. Alarms of German parachutists added to the spice of life at the fields and the pilots on occasion shot out Arab fires suspected of guiding in enemy raiders.

Neither quarters nor buildings were present at either airfield, the 47th digging in on hillsides around Youks and joining other units in the Thelepte ravine, a 40-minute walk from the aircraft dispersal area. The A-20 maintenance at Thelepte was probably typical of Twelfth Air Force practice at many an African airdrome in the early days. Spare parts were quickly exhausted and thereafter came from wrecks. Tin from "flimsies" took the place of aluminum for patching holes. Spare engines were obtained from damaged aircraft or engine cylinders were reringed, propeller blades were interchanged, and among other improvisations, large drums equipped with hand-driven fuel pumps and mounted on trucks were used to carry fuel from the five-gallon flimsies to the A-20's tanks. All work went on in the teeth of a high, cold wind with insufficient tools and equipment and in the constant expectation of enemy air attack.[57]

The A-20's and DB-7's were employed from both Youks and Thelepte--their targets at first determined by the British, later passed down from Twelfth Air Force Headquarters. Occasionally, in the early days when communications were bad, the fighters discovered profitable targets and fighter group headquarters developed the missions. From 14 to 30 December about half the targets faced British or French units on the northern front: Pont du Fahs, Mateur, Massicault, Sidi Tabet. But after the latter date no missions went north of Pont du Fahs. Altogether the DB-7's and A-20's attacked docks twice, shipping twice, airdromes on four occasions and railroad targets on nine. In late December and into January, as the number of Axis troops increased in the southern sector, seven missions were carried out against tanks and tank depots, camps, and other troop concentrations.[58]

Reconnaissance was an important if routine part of the fighters' duties, especially in the Medenine-Tripoli area where the P-38's could keep an eye on Rommel's dispositions and supply and often find profitable targets of opportunity. On 12 December, four P-38's were out over the Gafsa-Kebili-Gabes area, strafing and destroying four vehicles east of Kebili. Over Gabes five FW-190's were sighted far above and Lt. Virgil Smith, then the leading American fighter pilot in Northwest Africa, broke from his flight and climbed into the attack. The Focke-Wulf he singled out attempted to climb away, but the P-38 closed and fired and the German pilot bailed out. Two days later, the P-40's were on reconnaissance over Maknassy and Gabes. They came in over Gabes airdrome strafing a line of fighters thought to be Me-109's, destroying one, but were prevented by the intense flak from making a second attack. As it was, one P-40 did not return. Besides the folly of making more than one strafing attack on an AA-defended objective, Colonel Houyer's men were learning important lessons over Tunisia, their preceptors two squadrons of Me-109G's at Gabes. The P-40 pilots began basing their formations on the principal defense their plane offered--a quick turn--and since the Messerschmitts with their superior climb preferred the classic out-of-the-sun attack, the P-40's were distributed so that each pilot could look behind.[59]

The maiden mission of the 47th occurred on 14 December, two of its aircraft going out with 7 DB-7's against the marshalling yards at Sfax. Eight P-38's flew high cover and 10 P-40's were close in. The bombers dumped 34 x 500-lb. bombs on the yards, igniting a string of gasoline tank cars and leaving fires visible for 40 miles. In the afternoon, with P-38 escort, the DB-7's went back to the same target damaging buildings adjacent to the tracks.

On the 15th and 16th the DB-7's ran three missions against northern Tunisia and the 17th saw nine DB-7's with three A-20's over a landing ground near Sidi Tabet, 10 miles northwest of Tunis. Escort was by a dozen P-38's and as many Spits, evidently from Souk el Arba, which joined the formation over Le Kef. The bombing was reported as excellent, all 45 x 500-pounders in the perimeter of the field. Although three Me-109's attacked as the formation was leaving the target, all aircraft returned safely.[60]

During the next two days the Fighter Command's bombers attacked railroad yards at Sfax and Mateur and a landing ground northeast of the latter town. With the weather shutting down shortly thereafter, A-20's and DB-7's were kept idle until the end of December. The fighters, however, carried on the air war. Of a reported three Ju-88's attacking Tebessa and Youks on the 21st, two were destroyed by the P-38's, and a week later a P-38 of the 1st Fighter Group on patrol over Youks attacked one of three Me-109's approaching from the northeast. The Messerschmitt fled on the deck but after a chase to Le Kef, the P-38 closed and shot the intruder down.

On 30 December XII Fighter Command concentrated its efforts on Gabes and encountered stiff opposition. A dozen DB-7's escorted by as many P-38's of the 14th Group made the first attack--the target a troop encampment near the town. The bombers released 51 x 500-lb. and 6 x 300-lb. bombs and results were reported as good. The P-38's were fully occupied after the formation left Gabes. Four of them beat off five Me-109's after a 10-minute engagement. The remainder of the escort meanwhile was repulsing other interceptors, but three pilots who broke off in pursuit of the Messerschmitts did not return to base, amongst them Lt. Virgil Smith. Three-quarters of an hour after the DB-7's, eight A-20's took off for the Gabes airdrome, protected by 16 P-40's; the majority of their bombs fell, however, in a wood at the northeast corner of the field.

In the afternoon the DB-7's returned to blast the troop encampment with 200- and 300-pounders, encountering heavy flak at 12,000 feet that damaged three of the bombers, of which one crash-landed at base. Again the Luftwaffe made interception, but lost one Me-109 to the P-38 escort and another to the fire of a DB-7. The 47th Group terminated the day's activities with an attack on a gasoline dump in a wood at El Aouinet, nine miles northwest of Gabes. On the return, four of the dozen escorting P-40's broke off to attack tanks near El Guettar and a suspicious haystack northeast of Maknassy. On being strafed the haystack burned in a gratifying manner as though it had been camouflaging gasoline.[61]

Sousse bore the full weight of the attack on 31 December and again on 2 January. On the 31st two missions went out in the afternoon, the first to the railroad yards, which were bombed from 6,500 feet. Flak, heavy and light, intense and accurate, damaged two out of nine DB-7's, one crashing into the harbor, the other managing to return to base. The second attack fired the dock area on both sides of the harbor, but two more DB-7's were hit by the AA, which exploded one bomber in mid-air. On the 2d the 47th Group opened the assault by going in on the docks at 1,100 feet. As the seven A-20's and their P-40 escort were leaving the target, eight DB-7's approached at 9,800 and, amid intense flak, scored on the docks and the town, claiming a direct hit on a large merchant vessel. Later in the day, five DB-7's raided a troop concentration east of Sousse, reporting numerous bursts on a camp.[62]

On 3 January reconnoitering P-40's reported approximately 50 enemy tanks moving westward in the vicinity of Fondouk el Aouareb against the French front beyond Kairouan. All Fighter Command activity was directed to this target, almost 100 sorties being flown by various units. The Panzers were formidable opponents, quick to turn effective fire on low-flying aircraft, and effectively concealing themselves under trees, in bushes, and camouflaged in fields. Bombing and strafing went on almost continuously from 1100 hours and two tanks were destroyed, four left burning. The armor, however, went on to take Fondouk from the French.

Next day the harassment of the enemy force continued, but at high cost. Four A-20's took off, with 6 P-40's escorting, for a low-level attack--evidently against tanks at Cherichera. Two of the A-20's and two P-40's encountered three Me-109's and an FW-190, and both Bostons were lost. The high cover of four P-40's, moreover, lost two of their number when three more Me-109's materialized.[63]

The major enemy base of Kairouan, just behind Fondouk and Cherichera, was attacked several times during the next two days by the A-20's, but reports disagree as to the number of attacks and the identity of the targets, except that a troop concentration in the public gardens was bombed on the 7th. By 2 January, however, approximately 16 enemy aircraft were using the local landing ground and it is likely that this concentration attracted XII Fighter Command's attention. On the 8th, escorted by P-40's, the A-20's went down to Gabes on a tank-buster mission, the formation destroying one of four white-nosed Me-109's which disputed the passage.[64]

Internal Reorganization

The necessities of TORCH's widely spread amphibious landings dictated the initial organization of the Twelfth Air Force. General Cannon had brought XII Air Support Command into Morocco as an air task force, subordinate not to General Doolittle but to the Western Task Force commander, and a similar arrangement obtained as regards the Twelfth Air Force proper, which operated directly under Maj. Gen. Lloyd R. Fredendall's Center Task Force. As the French in western Algeria and Morocco capitulated en masse and as Spanish Morocco, despite recurrent alarms, remained quiet, the Center and Western Task Forces peaceably established contact in the hinterland on 24 November. Even prior to that date Twelfth Air Force organization began to shape itself for the new situation.[65]

First step was the order of 23 November, by which all units of the Twelfth Air Force were relieved from assignment to the task force commanders and given over to General Doolittle. The Twelfth's commander already realized that he had an unusual problem on his hands, one that could not be wholly met out of previous experience or current organizational doctrine. On 19 November, he was writing to General Arnold, summarizing the Twelfth's career since D-day and detailing plans for the future.[66]

His first concern was to position the principal part of his striking power for the Tunisian encounter. He hoped that the British would soon assign a definite sector in the forward area, a hope fulfilled when his DB-7's and P-38's took over at Youks.[67] The Twelfth Air Force, however, had duties beyond supporting the eastward push. Bases had to be prepared and maintained against the threat of hostile action via Spain or Spanish Morocco, and fighter cover and antisubmarine protection needed to be provided for the convoys to Casablanca and those threading the western Mediterranean.

To accomplish these ends, General Doolittle signified his intention of breaking the vast African area into districts, each to be assigned a small air force--a composite organization operating both fighters and bombers. XII Bomber Command was to be established at some point south of Bone, the exact site probably depending on the location of a suitable airdrome area. The Algiers region would comprise another district, and to the west of it, at Oran, XII Fighter Command would function. For the time being, XII Air Support Command was to remain at Casablanca, until the headquarters of the Fifth Army was established, as contemplated, at Oran.[68]

No immediate developments occurred, the delay possibly reflecting the general uncertainty as to just what forces were needed to contain Spanish Morocco and the specific difficulty of finding and constructing airbases. The first general reorganization came on 11 December, pursuant to General Order 8, and it followed out in a broad way General Doolittle's design as evinced in his 19 November letter. However, it was not a definitive step and ushered in a period when commands and wings were activated and shuffled in such a way as to tangle any discussion of Twelfth Air Force organization.

GO #8 set up five area commands. XII Bomber Command was established in the Telergma-Biskra region, its territory extending from Bougie east to the Tunisian border, with Colonel Phillips' headquarters at Constantine. This did not, however, disturb XII Fighter Command's advance echelon which retained responsibility for air defense of the Tebessa region and for any territory to be captured to the east. These jurisdictions proved firm compared to those created by GO #8 farther west.

In the Algiers area a Central Algerian Composite Wing was set up under Col. Paul L. Williams, the 51st Troop Carrier Wing to furnish the cadre. Although Colonel Williams took command and as many as three staff assignments were made, from all advices CACW never really operated. In the Oran area, embracing the territory from Cap Tenes to and including Oujda, Western Algerian Composite Wing was established. This wing was actually the rear echelon of XII Fighter Command, commanded from La Senia by XII Fighter Command's chief of staff, Col. Lawrence P. Hickey. A staff was drawn from Fighter Command, and WACW functioned until the advent of the air defense wings in February. In Morocco a Moroccan Composite Wing was set up, which entered into a series of rather intricate relationships with XII Air Support Command as a result of General Cannon's being commander of both organizations. Actually, MCW did not come to life under Col. Rosenham Beam until the end of December, XII ASC continuing to function in the interim.[69]

Although a certain amount of confusion ensued after the promulgation of GO #8, Brig. Gen. Delmar H. Dunton's XII Air Force Service Command (XII AFSC) was able to set up in agreement with that order, the elements of a stable organization. Its own order of 14 December merely legitimized three service area commands which were already operating in the areas controlled by Moroccan Composite Wing, Western Algerian Composite Wing, and XII Bomber Command. Except for such matters as the disposition of personnel assigned to service units and the operation of installations servicing more than one air force subcommand, these SAC's were under the command jurisdiction of the Twelfth Air Force subcommander concerned.

GO #10, 14 December, Headquarters, XII AFSC, created the Casablanca Service Area Command (Prov) under Col. Harold A. Bartron, the Oran Service Area Command (Prov) under Col. George H. Beverly, and the Constantine Service Area Command (Prov) under Col. Ray A. Dunn. Service units in the Central Algerian Composite Wing's area operated directly under Headquarters, XII AFSC, which had been moved from Oran to Algiers on 13 December. On 23 December the three SAC's were respectively redesignated 1st, 2d, and 3d Service Area Commands (Prov). With minor changes in designation and location XII AFSC organization remained substantially as above throughout the Tunisian campaign, although an attempt later was made to organize a fourth SAC for the Algiers area. Reflecting the decline in paratroop operations, on 5 January General Dunton was assigned the 51st Troop Carrier Wing and 10 days later his command was given the responsibility for air transport within the theater. The new assignment of the 51st was contested by the troop carrier units on the ground that it implied that they were merely service organizations. Not until February did they cease going directly to Twelfth Air Force Headquarters instead of channeling through XII AFSC.[70]

Some clues as to General Doolittle's thought on organization were furnished by Brig. Gen. Gordon P. Saville on his return from Africa early in January 1943. In an interview at Headquarters, Army Air Forces, General Saville outlined and defended the commander's over-all plans for the Twelfth. A basic division was to be made between the "striking force"--three bomb wings functioning in the forward sector--and a "holding corporation," that is a fighter command supervising XII Air Support Command and two air defence wings in the rear areas. All three of the fighter command's subordinate echelons would be prepared, as regards airdromes and logistics, to employ any part of the Twelfth Air Force needed to safeguard the Strait of Gibraltar.[71]

The key to the understanding of subsequent trends in the organization of the Twelfth Air Force lies, however, rather in General Eisenhower's appreciation of the strategic situation and his plans for applying effective force against the Axis in North Africa. In respect to Spanish Morocco and the Strait, his policy had been to weaken the components of the Fifth Army in order to help in the race

Tunis and to rely on the England-based Northern Task Force for insurance against hostile Spanish action. Moreover, when he was thwarted on the Medjerda route, he pulled out additional units of the Fifth Army, set them up as the U. S. II Corps, and planned to use them from central Tunisia against Rommel's line of communications.

Therefore, generally speaking, the next outstanding event in Twelfth Air Force organization occurred in early January--the replacement in the Tebessa area of XII Fighter Command by XII Air Support Command, which latter had been designated to cooperate with II Corps. So far as can be determined, XII Fighter Command's initial situation in the forward area was somewhat adventitious, an *ad hoc* arrangement to further a campaign believed at the time to be but a few weeks from its finish.[72]

XII Air Support Command's early career may be summarized as follows: from 11 November until 6 January it was relatively inactive, engaged in administration of the Moroccan area, in forming the Moroccan Composite Wing, and in preparing an air force contingent to discharge its obligation to the Fifth Army. During this period, pursuant to an order of 28 November, many of its combat units were taken from it and passed to the active front in the East. Upon General Cannon's transfer to the Bomber Command, XII ASC was briefly commanded by Colonel Beam (30 December-1 January) and Col. Peter S. Rask (1-10 January). On 10 January General Craig, who was to take the command into the Tunisian struggle, became CG.[73]

Meanwhile, on 5 January another reorganization was decreed and GO 8 was rescinded. XII Air Support Command was placed directly under Twelfth Air Force, "except when attached to other organizations," presumably ground organizations. XII Bomber Command remained undisturbed by the order, and the chief novelty was the replacement of the Moroccan, Western Algerian, and Central Algerian Composite Wings by the 2d, 1st, and 3d Air Defense Wings, respectively, upon the arrival of headquarters of these latter units in the theater. The ADW's were assigned directly to XII Fighter Command the headquarters of which retired from Tebessa to La Senia to administer them.[74]

The designs for American participation in the air defense of North Africa went back at least to 20 November, when a paper on the subject had been submitted to General Arnold. The plan specified that XII Fighter Command with four ADW's be responsible for the whole African coast from the environs of Casablanca to Tunis. The failure to capture Tunis scotched this project. Air defense plans then went through several modifications until the outline of the Tunisian battle became clear. Three headquarters and headquarters squadrons for air defense wings were set up in the United States in December, in the expectation that they would operate at Casablanca, Oran, and Algiers. The reorganization of 5 January made this design official, but it was later decided to leave Algiers to the British, the third wing eventually finding its way to the XII Air Support Command forward of Tebessa.

The Moroccan Composite Wing and Western Algerian Composite Wing continued to function until the headquarters for 1st and 2d ADW's arrived in the theater and were able to take over. The Headquarters and Headquarters Squadrons of the 1st and 2d came into Oran on 27 January; evidently plans had been changed, for the 1st then proceeded overland to Casablanca. Headquarters and Headquarters Squadron, 3d ADW, did not arrive until 21 February and on the 27th was still at the bivouac area near Oran. Commanding the 1st (Casablanca) ADW was Brig. Gen. Elwood R. Quesada, the 2d (Oran) Col. Davis D. Graves, and the 3d (eventually with XII Air Support Command) Col. Robert S. Israel.[75]

Chapter IV
THE DEVELOPMENT OF COMMAND AND STRATEGY

The Theater Air Force

In the consistently held view of the U. S. Army Air Forces, the strategic air bombardment of Germany was basic to any offensive against the European Axis. The ROUND-UP plan had been entirely consonant with this conception as it envisioned heavy strategic air action against Germany and German-held territory as a necessary precursor to a Continental landing. The air instrument of this strategy was the Eighth Air Force, created even prior to the adoption of the ROUND-UP plan, established in the convenient English base, and prepared for a task toward which USAAF training and thinking had been peculiarly bent.[1]

Upon the temporary abandonment of the cross-Channel strategy, the air offensive against Germany had been continued on the basis of an assurance by the CCS that resources would be available to the Eighth Air Force and the RAF for a "constantly increasing intensity of air attack on Germany."[2] Despite this assurance some uneasiness prevailed as to the effect of TORCH on what the RAF and USAAF alike considered their main and most profitable European objective.

On 20 August 1942 Sir Charles Portal communicated with General Arnold in this vein, begrudging Africa the two groups of heavy bombers which the Eighth was contributing to TORCH. He pointed out, as well, that after the Twelfth's requirements were satisfied, General Spaatz, commanding the Eighth, would be left with only four fighter groups for sweeps and escort. Although Sir Charles conceded TORCH's importance, he hoped that diversions to the Pacific could be cut down.[3]

Two days later General Spaatz was urging the build-up of his force in a letter to General Eisenhower. He made the points that the success of TORCH was largely dependent on Allied air supremacy and that the springs of German air power, unreachable from Africa, could be dried up from England. Moreover, a powerful air force in England was a convenient reservoir of strength for the air force in Africa. On the last point General Arnold's opinion coincided. He emphasized before the Joint Chiefs of Staff that Africa was inferior in air bases and logistical facilities and that only a limited number of units could be initially operated from that area, whereas the United Kingdom could support more air units than were presently available. In short, General Arnold also believed it wise to accumulate TORCH's aircraft reserves in England.[4]

On 21 October General Spaatz obtained from the TORCH commander definite assurances that his air force's power would not be vitiated by further diversions. General Eisenhower informed him that the whole Eighth must be considered as in support of TORCH and for that reason should not be rendered impotent. Moreover, the Allied chief remarked that after the completion of TORCH he would "in all probability" return to the United Kingdom to prepare for ROUND-UP. In the interim he was instructing Maj. Gen. Russell P. Hartle, who was to be his deputy in England, that the Eighth was not to be disturbed in its operations.[5]

Not a week later, General Eisenhower was fostering more ambitious plans for post-TORCH air forces. Assuming the availability of the African littoral, he planned to place a single command over all U. S. air units operating against the European Axis. This force, making use of bases "from Iceland to Iraq," could exploit the strategic mobility of the flight echelons of the air force. Moreover, such a unified command could expect to be more favored by the Combined Chiefs of Staff than two or three separate commands competing for resources to destroy Germany. More effective arguments could be brought against diversions to the Pacific.

General Eisenhower was explicit in his designs. He stated to General Spaatz that he intended to name him to the over-all command and to advocate the inclusion in that command of the U. S. Ninth Air Force. Anticipating that he might be able to put forward this proposal in a month's time, he instructed General Spaatz to be prepared to bring to him in 30 days, wherever he might be, a plan in the form of a cablegram to the Combined Chiefs of Staff.

General Spaatz accordingly made his arrangements. He counted on moving General Eaker up from CG, VIII Bomber Command to CG, Eighth Air Force, and on utilizing the Eighth Air Force staff as the nucleus of the Theater air force staff. He directed that plans to achieve the required mobility be immediately undertaken, and to Brig. Gen. Haywood S. Hansell, Jr., he gave the responsibility of preparing the cablegram called for by General Eisenhower.[6]

On 31 October General Spaatz reported the proposed reorganization to General Arnold, pointing out that it enabled heavy bombers to be shifted into as well as out of the United Kingdom, and remarking that it tended in the direction of the command setup previously suggested by the CG, AAF, a unified command of all British and American air forces on the European front. Headquarters, AAF, which had spent during the autumn a good portion of its time fighting the diversion of units to the Pacific, fell in with the plan.[7]

On 17 November, nine days after the landings in Africa, General Spaatz flew down to Gibraltar for conferences with Generals Eisenhower and Doolittle, bearing with him the detailed plans for the reorganization. Among the documents was a memorandum, "Organization of the Air Forces in ETOUSA," setting forth the rationale of the theater air force. The new TORCH air base area, linking geographically all U. S. air forces in the European theater and placing them in a position of mutual support with those in the Middle East, should be exploited by an overall air command which would concentrate the mass of its striking power against the chosen objective. And as to objectives, the memorandum reaffirmed that Germany was the principal enemy and that the United Kingdom was the only base area capable of supporting telling blows against her; an air war against Italy, although profitable, was distinctly second in priority, to be undertaken when the weather hampered England-based bombers.

According to General Spaatz' account, a preliminary conference was held with General Eisenhower and further discussion postponed until the Eighth Air Force commander had visited the theater. Brig. Gen. L. S. Kuter and General Hansell were left at Gibraltar to rewrite the plans for the proposed reorganization. A new memo on organization of the air forces in ETOUSA was prepared which omitted any reference to the priorities of Germany and Italy as targets for an air war. It is not too much to surmise that by this time General Eisenhower had discovered from the sentiments of higher echelons that he was not for a considerable time going back to the United Kingdom to prepare for ROUND-UP, and that an air war on Italy was a prime element in the current plans of the President and the Prime Minister.[8]

On 21 November General Spaatz returned to Gibraltar, and the reorganization was thrashed out. The gist of the plan was as follows: the CG, USAAF in ETO, would exercise his command of all U. S. Army Air Forces in the theater from the CP of the theater commander, where he would maintain a small staff. The commanders of the Eighth and Twelfth Air Forces would be his subordinates and he would advise the theater commander on matters concerning the USAAF, prepare plans for its employment, and coordinate strategic air operations and strategic plans with the RAF. The position of the Twelfth Air Force under the theater air force was to be as follows: until the African bases had been conquered and cooperation with the ground offensive ceased to be the major consideration in the Mediterranean, the Twelfth was to be attached to the TORCH forces. Once an air war on Italy became the major objective, control of the Twelfth or of its major components would revert to the theater air force commander.

General Eisenhower hesitated, preferring to wait until Tunisia had been freed from the Axis and the TORCH base area secured. However, at this juncture a letter from General Arnold arrived, suggesting that General Spaatz join AFHQ as air commander "in command of all [U. S.] air in England and Africa." General Eisenhower determined to proceed. Reorganization day was 1 December.⁹

Meanwhile, back in Washington, other plans were afoot that assumed the success of the African enterprise. On 18 November Prime Minister Churchill addressed a communication to the President on the subject of "Operations Subsequent to TORCH." Already, on the previous day, the Combined Staff Planners had been directed to undertake a study on the same general problem and the Prime Minister's communication was later referred to them. In the report of the CPS subcommittee, brought in on 27 November, and the discussions ensuing from it, there emerges a further view of the AAF's designs for the European war and of how General Spaatz' theater air force fitted into these designs.¹⁰

The document actually consisted of a majority and a minority report--the latter by the USAAF member, Col. R. P. Williams. The Prime Minister's able and vigorous letter had contemplated the exploitation of TORCH by further offensives in the Mediterranean area, a position with which President Roosevelt was in accord. With the Afrika Korps eliminated and an air war on Italy begun, Churchill found Sicily and Sardinia the logical next objectives, and of these Sicily the more profitable. He also discussed aid to Turkey and possible operations in the Aegean, Balkan, and Black Sea areas.[11] The CPS subcommittee's majority report followed out the Prime Minister's conception, concluding that TORCH should be exploited and that intensification of the war on Italy offered the best opportunities. Air, naval, and limited land operations might turn her into a first-class ulcer for Hitler. Meanwhile, plans for the seizure of Sicily should be initiated forthwith under General Eisenhower's direction.

To this reasoning Colonel Williams presented a 20-page demurrer. He weighed all operations looking towards the exploitation of TORCH against what he considered to be the basic concept of Allied war policy: an air offensive against Germany's industrial heart followed by a ROUND-UP type invasion. Consequently, he characterized assaults on Sicily or Sardinia as diversionary and Balkan operations in addition as logistically impossible. He advocated drawing up plans for both Sicily and Sardinia, in case subsequent events made their seizure advisable, but any such attacks should be timed for late fall or winter when the extensive support aviation could be best spared from operations out of England. Denying that the exploitation of TORCH was an immediate priority, he proposed to integrate North Africa with the ROUND-UP strategy. Therefore the United Kingdom and North Africa should be preserved as one theater and, once suitable base areas had been prepared in Africa, an extremely flexible and economical air arm should be set up on the perimeter of Festung Europa. Squadrons operating with minimum maintenance personnel could move between the United Kingdom and North Africa and shuttle between African airdromes for the purpose of satisfying such requirements as the strategic air offensive against Germany, normal reconnaissance, and support of invasions of Sicily, Sardinia, or Spanish Morocco.

Colonel Williams was not unaware of the capabilities of the African base area. Italy could be punished by both medium and heavy bombers to a degree that might paralyze her war effort. Counter-air force action, fighter cover, and antisubmarine sorties provided from Tunisia could reopen the Mediterranean to Allied convoys. Any subsequent descent on Sicily would be facilitated by an interim air war on the peninsula. But nothing changed the premise, "The heart of Germany's capacity to wage war is in Germany."[12]

On 30 November the CPS considered the report of its subcommittee and became mired in the perennial subject of the degree of security needed for the IOC through the Gibraltar Strait. The American members considered the narrow waterway overperilous in case of a German incursion into Spain, the British insisting that it could be kept open by air cover from the southern shore. In the meeting was Brig. Gen. Orvil A. Anderson, the Assistant Chief of Air Staff, Plans. His comment was that the subject report failed to bring out the alternatives to the Mediterranean operations.[13]

On 3 December the CPS again took up the report, but unable to come to any conclusion, referred it back to the subcommittee. On 8 December the subcommittee communicated that, in the absence of a restatement of the global strategic concept of the United Nations, it could not reconcile the various divergent views. The upshot was that the CPS finally advised the CCS that it could not reach an agreement without an accepted over-all strategic concept.[14]

The "various divergent views" of the CPS membership which its subcommittee had been unable to reconcile were embodied in four memoranda, prepared respectively by the British members, some of the U. S. Army members, the USAAF members, and the U. S. Navy air members. Those of the British and of the U. S. Army members accepted the continuance of the Mediterranean strategy and were mainly different in their estimates of the security of the life line through Gibraltar.

The USAAF memo, however, considered further Mediterranean amphibious operations inconclusive and diversionary and that TORCH could best be exploited by the exercise of air power from the new bases. The memorandum specifically recommended that "the global strategic concept defining the air offensive from the United Kingdom followed by invasion across the English Channel as the major British-American effort be reaffirmed," and "that this strategic plan be reevaluated without delay with a view to determination of a target date for the initiation of the land invasion."[15]

In the interim, the organization of the theater air force had proceeded, outwardly, according to plan. General Spaatz arrived at Algiers and on 5 December was announced as Acting Deputy Commander in Chief for Air, Allied Force. On 1 December General Eaker succeeded him as commander of the Eighth. In actuality, however, the logic of a theater air force was being called into question by the turn of events.[16]

As conceived in October and November 1942 by Generals Eisenhower and Spaatz, the theater air force organization was predicated on an immediate return to the ROUND-UP strategy, once TORCH was completed. Not only was TORCH considerably incomplete by the first week in December, but, since 18 November at least, the President and Prime Minister, if not their staffs, had been in substantial agreement that the Mediterranean strategy would be continued after the securing of the North African littoral. Therefore the theater air force, although its rationale had been shifted somewhat with the changing situation, took on an unreal tinge in the swirling strategic fogs of late 1942.

The Genesis of the Northwest African Air Forces

More than the theater air force command, however, had been disjointed by the failure to clear Tunisia. General Spaatz came on the scene at a time when the air command arrangements in Africa had themselves developed serious shortcomings. By the TORCH plan the Twelfth

Air Force and the Eastern Air Command initially had been given separate tasks and areas of responsibility. The EAC was to cooperate with the First Army's drive for Tunis, and the Twelfth was to aid the Fifth Army in the pacification of Algeria and Morocco and in any action made necessary by a hostile Spain. It was not anticipated that the two air forces would operate from the same areas until some six weeks or two months after D-day. Such integration of their efforts as might be necessary was to be accomplished from AFHQ, where a G-3 for air, Air Vice Marshal A.P.M. Saunders, had been installed.

The French, after the battles at Oran and Casablanca, had needed no further pacification and the Spaniards had committed no overt acts. The Twelfth therefore had been thrown into the Tunisian struggle, which far from proving a prelude to Rommel's entrapment, promised to provide a most serious test for Allied aims. Once removed to Algiers, AFHQ lost something of its combined nature. Eisenhower set up headquarters in the St. George Hotel; Admiral Cunningham, the naval commander, repaired aboard ship, and Air Marshal Welsh to Maison Carree, six miles outside the city. General Doolittle, who at least had moved in from Oran, maintained still another separate headquarters in Algiers. Out at Philippeville, Air Marshal Welsh was represented at General Anderson's CP by his senior air staff officer (SASO), Air Commodore Lawson. This dispersion of headquarters might have been borne had communications been adequate, but unhappily communications were appalling and General Doolittle and Air Marshal Welsh frequently were forced to travel considerable distances for personal conferences.

With the Twelfth and the EAC both in the battle area, where airdromes were few, the LOC was creaking, and the weather atrocious. General Eisenhower initially directed that Welsh effect the integration of the two air forces. This was logical enough, since it was on the air marshal's territory and resources that the Twelfth was impinging. However, since Welsh could not command the American squadrons, missions had to be arranged by constant consultation with General Doolittle, and misapprehensions even arose as to the employment of the Youks aircraft, control of which had been given over entirely to the First Army. Thus, as Eisenhower's deputy for air, General Spaatz found himself with a task fully as important as that he originally intended to perform at AFEQ.

The COS had taken up the question of air command in the Mediterranean on 19 November and asked for the views of all interested parties. Moreover, the Commanders in Chief, Middle East, had earlier studied the problem on the assumption that the Mediterranean would be the scene of the United Nations' major effort in 1943. Even in November integration of the Allied squadrons cooperating with the First Army was an inter-theater affair. RAF, Malta, hitting hard at the Axis bridgehead, lay under the jurisdiction of Middle East, and the solution advanced by the ACC, ME, Air Marshal Tedder, was a unified air command for the whole Mediterranean. It is likely that the substance of Tedder's views was urged upon AFEQ in early December by the British

Chiefs of Staff, but General Eisenhower objected to a thoroughgoing reorganization of command in the midst of battle. He wished to postpone the question until Tunisia had been cleared, although he admitted that the British plans were sound. He was forced, however, at the same time, to represent General Spaatz' recent appointment as a stopgap measure, in no way interfering with the CCS prerogatives of deciding on the eventual organization of air command in the Mediterranean.

Throughout December, then, General Spaatz, without command functions, labored to integrate the efforts of the Twelfth and Eastern Air Command and performed such tasks as that of dividing replacements between the Eighth and the Twelfth. The closest cooperation was maintained with RAF, ME, and Air Marshal Tedder attended organization conferences at AFHQ. What he observed there only confirmed him in the belief that over-all command was a necessity. Finally, at the end of that rainy December which buried hopes for the immediate capture of Tunis, General Eisenhower took advantage of the lull in the ground battle to straighten out his air command situation.[17]

The British had previously suggested that Air Marshal Tedder be made air commander with operational control of all bombers in the Mediterranean theater. Since, however, General Eisenhower considered that Tedder could not serve two ground commanders and that it was entirely essential that his air commander have control over the Eighth Air Force as well, he determined to avoid the issue by proposing General Spaatz as air commander for the TORCH area, entrusting the integration of the African bomber effort temporarily to his good relations with RAF, ME, and to the final establishment of a single air command for the theater. He hoped that the necessity of regarding the United Kingdom-TORCH-Middle East Area as one, so far as U. S. long-range bombers were concerned, would be recognized in the final reckoning.

On 31 December, therefore, he proposed to the CCS that General Spaatz be set up directly under AFHQ as commander of the TORCH air forces, on the ground that the utilization of British and American air units in the same area required such a step. He left the full unification of air effort in the theater to later decision by the Combined Chiefs. The reaction of the British Chiefs was favorable. They agreed to accept General Spaatz as commander of the RAF in the TORCH area, without prejudice to any later CCS decision to set up a unified air command for the whole Mediterranean, which they considered the best solution. The British Chiefs stated, however, that they wished to establish an organization in northwest Africa which would provide adequately not only for strategic bombing but for support of land and sea forces, general reconnaissance, and night fighting, in all of which they considered the RAF especially experienced. They proposed therefore that General Spaatz' Chief of Staff be an RAF officer and that there also be a senior RAF officer on his staff specially qualified in maintenance and supply.

As to the subdivisions of the unified air force, the British envisioned that they should comprise both American and British units grouped according to their functions, tactical requirements, and logistic possibilities. One subcommand would control heavy and medium bombers and escort fighters and engage in strategic bombing under an American commander. A second, under British command, would employ general reconnaissance and day and night fighter aircraft for port defense, protection of shipping, and cooperation with the Royal Navy. Lastly, a third subcommand, likewise under an RAF officer, would devote itself to cooperation with ground forces. Attached to it would be light bombers, Army cooperation squadrons, and fighters. Photo-reconnaissance aircraft probably, thought the British, were best retained under direct control of air headquarters with a forward detachment possibly operating under the ground-cooperation command.[18]

On 4 January General Eisenhower dispatched a cable to the CCS and the British Chiefs of Staff reporting his essential agreement with the latter's plan. However, for the present he meant to preserve the continuity of the Eastern Air Command and the Twelfth Air Force. The old organizations had already solved many of the difficult administrative problems peculiar to the theater, and the areas in which AFHQ was currently interested with respect to ground operations were widely separated. In general accord with the British plan were the functions he intended assigning to the two air forces. EAC was to control a general reconnaissance and air striking force to hit shipping at sea and a day and night fighter force to defend the ports and back areas. Through a subordinate commander EAC was responsible for close cover and cooperation with the First Army. To the Twelfth was assigned the task of carrying out strategic bombardment with heavy and medium bombers and the double duty of cooperation with American ground forces in Tunisia, and if need be, in Morocco.

In closing, General Eisenhower stated that, in view of the minor differences between his plan and that of the British Chiefs of Staff and because of the necessity of immediate action, he was organizing forthwith. He was as good as his word. On 5 January the Allied Air Force was activated and General Spaatz passed from his position as air adviser to General Eisenhower to air commander. Air Vice Marshal J. M. Robb became his chief of staff. As to his duties, General Spaatz received on the same day a directive which set forth his peculiar position. He was to coordinate the operations of the Eighth with those of the Allied Air Force. He was to cooperate with RAF, ME, and mediate between the Eighth, the Twelfth, and the Eastern Air Command with respect to replacement aircraft. The Allied Air Force thus became the link between the U. S. theater air force which had been projected for the post-TORCH period and the Northwest African Air Forces which emerged later as the answer to the organizational needs of the continuing African campaign.[19]

That Allied Air Force was a stopgap and a compromise should not obscure its merits. Most obvious of these was the placing of a common commander over the Twelfth and the EAC.* Thereby it ended the

---

* "One principal difficulty has resulted from the fact that we did not have a Single Command in the areas from which we operate."--General Doolittle to Staff Meeting, Twelfth Air Force, 21 Dec. 1942. Italics in original.

de jure separation of the two air forces decreed by the the TORCH plan--a separation long since rendered anomalous by the course of events in Africa. It satisfied General Eisenhower's conviction that the Eighth and Twelfth Air Forces were both necessary to the fortunes of TORCH. It provided a workable and sorely needed organization until the President, the Prime Minister, and the Combined Chiefs would choose definitely between ROUND-UP and the exploitation of TORCH. It could be developed to conform with either choice.

The odds against immediate initiation of ROUND-UP, however, were lengthening. The air planners in Washington had seen any chance of the immediate organization of its corollary theater air force stymied by the tenacious Axis lodgment in Tunisia. Beyond Allied Air Force, moreover, they saw other plans emergent--plans for an over-all Mediterranean air command, plans which anticipated a major effort against the "underbelly" and which foreshadowed the Casablanca decision to come. Small wonder then that AC/AS, Plans, after a considered view of the command developments, commented that "they looked to unified Anglo-American air command throughout the Mediterranean with particular focus on the Tunisian struggle--to the partial eclipse of our over-all strategic plan for European operations." A better summation of the pertinent decisions at Casablanca could hardly be found.[20]

On 14 January, the President and the Prime Minister came together at Anfa villa on the outskirts of Casablanca. There for 10 days the state of the war and designs for its vigorous prosecution were considered in the wide terms of global strategy, the task not being lightened by the nonattendance of the U.S.S.R. In the nature of the case, plans and prospects for the African campaign played a leading role in the discussions.

Most important strategically was the decision to exploit the African lodgment and deployment by further Mediterranean offensives. The previous lack of such a decision at the highest level had exercised a muddying effect on contemporary planning--witness the difficulties of the CPS in Washington and the abortive plan for an over-all U. S. air force in ETOUSA. The step was finally taken in spite of the U. S. Joint Chiefs' preference for a 1943 cross-Channel operation, but the JCS were able in return to establish their contention that Sicily, not Sardinia, was the proper next objective in the Mediterranean.[21]

In accordance with the over-all strategic decision and in view of the progressive *de facto* fusion of the Middle East and North African theaters, the CCS at Casablanca prescribed new command arrangements for the Mediterranean. For HUSKY, the projected Sicilian operation, the present Naval Commander X Force, Fleet Admiral Cunningham, was to assume the title of Commander in Chief, Mediterranean, the present C-in-C, Mediterranean, to become C-in-C, Levant. A similar arrangement was reached in regard to the land forces. At an unstipulated time after the Eighth Army had crossed the Tunisian frontier, General Alexander was to be designated General Eisenhower's Deputy Commander in Chief and the Eighth Army would pass to AFHQ's command. Subject to General Eisenhower's approval, General Alexander's immediate task thereafter would be to command all Allied ground forces on the Tunisian front.[32]

The CCS also agreed on an over-all air command for the Mediterranean by adopting the substance of the British proposals. As Air C-in-C, Mediterranean, Sir Arthur Tedder was chosen. Under him were to be two principal subordinates, the ACC-in-C, Northwest Africa (General Spaatz) and the ACC-in-C, Middle East (Air Chief Marshal Sir Sholto Douglas). The organization of General Spaatz' command, the future NAAF, was specifically laid down.

General Spaatz was to have at his disposal the Western Desert Air Force, the Twelfth Air Force, and the Eastern Air Command. From these elements he was required by the CCS to form three main sub-commands—a heavy and medium bomber force with appropriate escort fighters, a coastal air force for port and shipping protection, and a tactical air force or air support command. The last was to work in conjunction with General Alexander and to comprise the three air detachments cooperating with the main ground forces ringing the Axis bridgehead, the British First and Eighth Armies, and the U. S. II Corps. Evidently, agreement had been reached on the commander of this tactical air force—Air Marshal Sir Arthur Coningham, currently heading Western Desert Air Force. These arrangements were in essence a development of the plan agreed to by General Eisenhower on 4 January, just before he activated the Allied Air Force. Minor details were left to Air Marshal Tedder and the date for implementing the new organization was not specified, but hereafter air organization in Northwest Africa proceeded according to the master plan.²³

So far as the Eighth Air Force was concerned, the Anfa hilltop called a halt to its "parlous days," as an VIII Bomber Command history later dubbed the waning months of 1942 and the early months of 1943. The Eighth had been suffering from the lack of a clear-cut, long-term directive for its work, the lack of replacement aircraft and crews, the lack of good bombing weather, and the necessities of supporting TORCH. Repair of its bombers had waited upon the readying of the Twelfth's aircraft with the result that serviceability was low and abortives were high. The top priority targets were the submarine pens in the Bay of Biscay, which meant that VIII Bomber Command was pinned down to highly defended targets.

At Casablanca, this crisis was met and passed. General Eaker was called down from England and was able to convince Winston Churchill that the Eighth's ineffectiveness of recent months was no fault of its own and that the proposed conversion of its bombers to night operations in concert with the RAF would be impracticable and wasteful. On 21 January, the COS issued a directive on the bomber offensive from the United Kingdom. This document reaffirmed the strategic bombing policy which had founded the Eighth, assured the continuance of daylight bombing from the United Kingdom, and freed General Eaker's force to a large extent from the exigencies of aiding TORCH and from dependence on TORCH's priority for the resources to continue its work.

Hereafter the Eighth went its own way in England.[24]

The formal separation of England and Africa came later when Headquarters, North African Theater of Operations, United States Army, was established on 4 February under General Eisenhower's command. American forces in England remained in ETOUSA and an air force man, Lt. Gen. Frank M. Andrews, was appointed CG. The setting up of NATOUSA symbolized and implemented the Casablanca decision that the imminent attempt to break into the European fortress was to be made in the Mediterranean, from the African springboard. From England, for the time being, only an air offensive would be mounted.[25]

Chapter V
AIR-GROUND COOPERATION IN CENTRAL TUNISIA

Operation SATIN

New Year's Day of 1943 found Rommel's divisions in the neighborhood of Buerat, some 250 miles west of El Agheila, where the Wadi Zemzem and adjacent coastal marshes held out some hope of delaying the oncoming British Eighth Army. The Afrika Korps had had its rear punished two weeks before at Wadi Matratin, but for the most part it had made its way safely and in extreme haste from El Agheila, leaving hosts of mines and booby traps in its wake. In fact, the Korps retreated so rapidly that first the Ninth Air Force's medium and then its fighters ran out of bombing targets, practiced though they were in exploiting the rapid advance of the army.[1]

In Tunisia, General Eisenhower was occupied in separating, so far as possible, the supply lines of his main forces. The British First Army was based at much-bombed Bone, drawing its sustenance through La Calle and Souk Ahras. Twelfth Air Force was based on Philippeville, its supplies going by rail and road directly to the south. II Corps, newly arriving at the front, was based back at Oran and Algiers; via the execrable rail line running east, its stores came to Constantine and thence by metre-gauge railway to the advance depots at Tebessa.

II Corps, detached from the Center Task Force at Oran, embodied Allied Force's hopes of breaking the deadlock which had existed since early December. After it had become apparent that "General Mud" would not relax his grip on the First Army sector until at least March, General Eisenhower had turned his attention to central Tunisia, whence an attack could be mounted on the communications between Rommel and Von Arnim. Fifth Army Headquarters commenced the planning in December and on New Year's Day II Corps' staff assembled in Algiers to prepare for Operation SATIN.[3]

According to II Corps' report, three alternative plans were drawn up, all requiring the SATIN Task Force, of which the U. S. 1st Armored Division was the core, to be concentrated forward of Tebessa. In Plan A, Sfax was to be taken and the STF would then operate northwards against Sousse. Plan B contemplated the capture of Gabes and a northward movement against Sfax. By Plan C, Kairouan would be taken as preliminary to an advance on Sousse. The choice among these plans devolved on General Eisenhower; he seems to have decided first on a variant of "A," then on "B." Successfully carried out, either would split the Axis forces into two pockets, and even if Sfax could not be held, temporary occupation would be of substantial aid to the Eighth Army, for the bulk of Rommel's supplies came down to Sfax by rail from Tunis and Bizerte.[3]

The project had its risks. In the first instance, success depended on a coordinated attack by the Eighth Army on the Mareth Line, the old French works in which Rommel was expected to make his stand. Failing such a conjuncture, the Afrika Korps could easily detach enough strength to jeopardize SATIN's southern flank and its communications with Algeria.

SATIN's northern flank was similarly vulnerable to a known concentration of enemy armor around Kairouan. General Eisenhower realized that the First Army would have to be employed simultaneously in local attacks to contain Von Arnim in the north, although he was reluctant to use in this way a force building for decisive action in the spring. SATIN also presented difficulties on the logistical side. Once east of the Tebessa railheads, all supplies would have to proceed by motor transport 160 miles to the sea. To get the necessary vehicles, truck units were transferred from port and base areas, and congestion on the quays was accepted. It was hoped that upon Sfax's capture maintenance could be considerably eased by dint of Middle East convoys.[4]

General Eisenhower's first choice for the SATIN commander was General Clark, but he needed him to head the Fifth Army, activated at Oujda on 5 January. Therefore, on 1 January, he appointed General Fredendall to the command of II Corps, which included the 1st Armored Division, the 701st TD Battalion, the 443d CA Battalion, and the 26th Regimental Combat Team plus the 5th FA Battalion and the 601st TD Battalion. Additionally, under General Fredendall's command were the French Constantine Division and a British paratroop brigade.

The orders for air support also went forward on 1 January. Air Marshal Welsh was to provide assistance from 242 Group, insofar as it was not committed at the time to the First Army, but the main burden lay with XII Air Support Command, commanded by General Craig at Tebessa. XII ASC became responsible not only for cooperation with II Corps but for meeting requests from French elements for aid south of an east-west line through Dechret bou Dabouss, these requests to be passed through General Fredendall. Moreover, XII ASC was empowered to arrange mutual assistance with 242 Group to the north.[5]

On 9 January, General Craig's air establishment consisted of two understrength squadrons of the 33d Fighter Group and the entire 47th Light Bombardment Group. The P-38's of the 14th Group were in process of being withdrawn. The airdrome situation had been much improved. Besides Youks, inclined to mud, there were the two all-weather fields at Thelepte and forward landing grounds at Gafsa and Sbeitla. A good part of this development represented the work of the 883th Airborne Engineer Company (Avn) which, besides contributing to the establishment of some of the above fields, had constructed two runways at Tebessa, one at Le Kouif, and hardstands at Kalaa Djerda. In addition, if SATIN broke through to the coast, General Craig could count on airdromes at Gabes and Sfax.

Craig, however, was not overimpressed with his command. On the 9th, he was cabling Twelfth Air Force Headquarters, calling attention to the low serviceability of the 33d Group and the "ineffectiveness" of the 47th, which he considered poorly trained in all respects. In fact, he recommended that the 47th be withdrawn before SATIN began and replaced by a P-39 group equipped with 37-mm. cannon. He also wished headquarters to clarify the status of the Lafayette Escadrille, scheduled shortly to arrive in his area, as the impression prevailed at Tebessa that the French Army would control this unit. Twelfth Air

Force replied that a squadron of 20-mm.-equipped P-39's was on the way to XII ASC, but that it could not agree to the relief of the 47th Group. Two days later, after he had attended a conference at II Corps headquarters at Constantine and had the operation outlined to him, General Craig came to the conclusion that he had not enough air power to perform his mission. He considered that four fully operational fighter squadrons represented the minimum for effective support of SATIN. Twelfth Air Force wired back that strength in excess of four squadrons would be available to XII ASC by D-day. General Doolittle, however, concurred in General Craig's plan to conserve his operational strength for the forthcoming test.[6]

Perhaps reflecting this conservation policy, XII ASC was relatively inactive, except for normal reconnaissance, in the 10 days from 8 to 18 January. II Corps was still assembling in the forward area, and the Germans and Italians made no immediate move. General Craig began receiving the reinforcements he had asked for: the 4th Squadron of the 52d Group (Spitfires) and the 91st and the 92d Squadrons of the 81st Group (P-39's) came into Thelepte before 20 January; the Lafayette Escadrille also arrived and General Craig was confirmed in his command of the unit. The only operations of note took place on the 10th. The enterprising Major Cochran, then commanding the 33d Group's 58th Squadron, dropped a 500-pound bomb squarely on German headquarters at the Hotel Splendide in Kairouan, demolishing the building, and on the same day the A-20's went down to Kebili, beyond the Chott Djerid.

Eight of them with a half-dozen escorting P-40's made a low-level attack on the military camp; the Bostons dropped 44 x 100-pounders, and both bombers and fighters strafed the town.[7]

Whatever General Craig thought of XII ASC's potentialities with respect to SATIN, as it turned out his command was not required to carry through the plan. General Eisenhower attended the Casablanca conference for only one day, 15 January; he reported on the progress of the Tunisian campaign and conferred with General Alexander. From the latter, he received an appreciation of the Eighth Army's probable schedule. General Montgomery did not expect to reach Tripoli before late January or to be in position to attack the Mareth Line before mid-February. A coordinated attack on the SATIN D-day, 23 January, was impossible. General Eisenhower, in any case, had not been over-enthusiastic about the project, and on 17 January he wired the Commanders in Chief, Middle East, that they could cancel their arrangements for convoys to Sfax or Gabes. He did not, however, propose to adopt a purely defensive attitude in central Tunisia and instructed II Corps to act as aggressively as possible against the Axis communications without committing its main forces.[8]

The Allied Air Support Command

Necessary to any account of the involved series of actions which began in central Tunisia in the last half of January is a glance at the relevant Tunisian topography, rather involved in itself. The most prominent military feature of the region is the Grand Dorsal system which begins by furnishing the southern boundary of the Tunis plain and extends from Cap Bon on the north to the Chotts, the salt lakes to the west of Gabes. In the vicinity of Pont du Fahs, two ranges of the Grand Dorsal become apparent, with the valleys between running in a generally southwest to northeast direction. The Eastern Dorsal stretches southward to the Chotts, with passes at Fondouk, Faid, Maknassy, and Gafsa, in that order. The Western Dorsal parallels it, but bends rather farther to the west as it approaches the Chotts. In the passes and the empty valleys between these rugged systems the battles of central Tunisia were fought.[9]

In mid-December, General Giraud had suggested to AFHQ that the French XIX Corps take over the defense of the Eastern Dorsal. The proposal had its merits: the slim American and British forces needed assistance; the step had definite political and morale values; and the mountains seemed the only terrain where the French could be safely employed. By mid-January, however, when the French sector had assumed crucial importance as furnishing the only link between the First Army and II Corps, it became apparent that the link was weak. The French suffered from bad morale, "appalling" lack of equipment, and the initial unwillingness of Generals Barré and Juin to be subordinated to the First Army, which alone had the signal communications to control the entire front. Consequently, General Eisenhower was forced to take personal command from a CP at Constantine.

No one was more aware of the weak link than Field Marshal Erwin Rommel. Late in December before II Corps had arrived at the front, AFHQ was poring over a captured document dated 16 December, Rommel's "Appreciation of Situation." Therein, the Desert Fox discussed the Allied weaknesses of communications and supply in central Tunisia, the possible infirmities of Allied command, and the three French divisions facing Gabes and Sousse, which he characterized as "ill-equipped and of doubtful morale." To exploit the situation, he proposed to hold or delay the Eighth Army in Tripolitania with two divisions, mine fields, and fighter cover, and to strike via Gabes into Gafsa and Tebessa with his ultimate objectives Philippeville and Bone. Rommel's "Appreciation" possibly had something to do with General Eisenhower's reluctance to employ the SATIN plan, and at Anfa the Commander in Chief had emphasized the danger in the French sector and pleaded for arms for his poorly-equipped ally.

On the evening of 17 January, II Corps began moving up from the Constantine-Guelma area; already battalions of American infantry were at Kasserine and Gafsa. Facing the corps in the sector from Fondouk to Mahmassey was the equivalent of one strong division of mixed German and Italian infantry and an armored force possessing about 100 to 115 light and medium tanks, exclusive of the 10th Panzer Division north of Kairouan. On 18 January the Germans struck.[10]

The blow fell at the junction of the French and British sectors in the Bou Arada-Pont du Fahs area, the main attack threatening to

flow down the Robaa valley and cut off the French positions in the
mountains to the east. As the French drew back, the British and Americans
began to come to their aid, with detachments of the British 6th Armored
Division and Combat Command B of the U. S. 1st Armored. Moreover, an
American reserve force was directed to Maktar. By the 19th the
British had begun to exert pressure on the enemy flank at Bou Arada.
Nevertheless the Germans were able to penetrate far down the valley
and join two separate columns at Robaa village.

On 20 January another attack developed. The Germans stormed
Djebel Chirich, controlling the entrance to the Ousseltia valley, east
of and paralleling the Robaa valley, and once again drove down the
valley floor, isolating the French in the Eastern Dorsal. During the
night enemy detachments reached Ousseltia village. By the 22d the
situation had somewhat improved, with the 6th Armored establishing itself on the Robaa-Pont du Fahs road and Combat Command B moving up the
Ousseltia valley itself. Next day under cover of Combat Command B the
French were able to extricate themselves from the Eastern Dorsal north
of the Ousseltia-Kairouan road. By 25 January the enemy attack was
spent.[11]

The Axis assault on XIX Corps exposed the weakness of the air
"support" doctrines then in use along the Allied front. During the
first three days of the Robaa-Ousseltia action, XII ASC did not fly any
missions in the area, nor were its aircraft especially active on its own
front. The fighting lay north of the Dechret bou Dabouss line beyond

ROBAA AND OUSSELTIA ACTIONS

which the RAF was responsible and 242 Group had obliged by laying on fighterbomber sorties against such targets as the Germans and Italians presented. However, II Corps, which controlled XII ASC, at one point refused XIX Corps' request for air reconnaissance on the grounds that it had no responsibilities or interest in the area. It was true that about 70 miles of rugged terrain separated the two ground organizations, but such a distance was of course well within the range of General Craig's aircraft.[12]

On 22 January Spaatz dispatched to Tedder a message which began "Air support situation critical." He informed his chief-to-be that he was forced to implement part of the Casablanca-approved organization immediately, that General Kuter would be assigned as acting commander of a coordinating air-support organization until Air Marshal Coningham could arrive, and that the latter's early arrival was of the utmost importance. General Kuter's mission was to control the twin organizations, XII ASC and 242 Group, and cooperate with General Anderson who, in the emergency, had been given command of II and XIX Corps as well as the First Army. Additionally, on 21 January, Col. Paul L. Williams succeeded General Craig as commander of XII ASC.[13]

Kuter had formerly commanded the 1st Bomb Wing of the Eighth Air Force. Late in December General Spaatz had requested his transfer to Africa as a replacement for General Craig, who was then going forward with XII ASC. Kuter was subsequently announced as A-3 of Allied Air Force. On 22 January, General Kuter had his directive from Spaatz, and by the 23d had a cable address and a chief of staff, Col. John DeF.

Barker, at First Army headquarters in Constantine. His organization was known as the Allied Air Support Command and was the lineal ancestor of the Northwest African Tactical Air Force. By 25 January Allied Air Support Command was in operation, passing bombing requests back to Twelfth Air Force and Eastern Air Command.[14]

After 25 January the Allies were able to stabilize the situation in the Ousseltia valley, with Combat Command B, under Brig. Gen. P. L. Robinett, patrolling north from Ousseltia. On 26 January the 26th Regimental Combat Team attacked Kairouan Pass in the Ousseltia valley and took 400 Italian prisoners. The Germans retired up the valley, strewed it with mines, and went on the defensive in the high ground at its northern end. Until rain curtailed activity after the 24th, XII ASC was able to give somewhat more effective aid than during the first days of the operation. On the 22d, 10 P-39's of the 81st Group, 10 P-40's of the 33d, and a half-dozen P-40's of the Lafayette Escadrille had swept the Ousseltia valley, strafing tanks, trucks, and machine-gun positions, losing one P-40 in the process. In the afternoon, a dozen A-20's bombed a tank depot 17 miles NW of Ousseltia with GP's and incendiaries, escort consisting of 23 P-39's and P-40's. Next day an attack coordinated with the ground forces was laid on, the targets being heavy batteries, machine-gun positions, and two companies of infantry. A half-dozen escorted A-20's participated, dropping 4 x 500-lb., 8 x 300-lb., 9 x 100-lb. GP's, and 8 x 120-lb. frag clusters from 8,000 feet. Prisoners stated that two ammunition dumps were destroyed by the bombing.[15]

By 26 January the operational strength of XII ASC had been built to 52 P-40's, 25 P-39's, 27 A-20's, and 8 B-?'s. However, of the units making up this considerable force only the 33d Group seems to have been altogether equal to its task. The 47th Group had to contend with certain defects in its training and equipment and the new arrivals, the Lafayette Escadrille and the 81st Fighter, also labored under diverse handicaps.[16]

The presence of the Lafayette Escadrille on the Tunisian front came as a direct result of General Cannon's conviction that some use should be made of the numerous French Army pilots in Africa. His suggestion was taken up in higher headquarters and the Escadrille was furnished with P-40F's belonging to the 33d Group; the resulting shortage in the 33d had to be made up by diverting at Accra 20 P-40's destined for the Middle East. The French made an inauspicious beginning when two of their noncoms promptly flew their P-40's to France, to be enthusiastically received by the Vichyites. Without equipment or ground echelon, the Lafayette Escadrille went up to Thelepte where it was shortly assigned to airdrome patrol. The unit was commanded by Maj. Korstia Rosanoff, aged 37 or 38 and with about 3,000 flying hours to his credit. Major Rosanoff showed no disposition to listen to Major Cochran or others who had learned to use the P-40 in actual combat. The Lafayette Escadrille was interested in la chasse pure, insisted on flying a classical "V" and tried to climb into the sun against the ME-109G's. The result was that it knocked itself out in a very few days.[17]

For the background of the 81st Group, it is necessary to go back to August 1942. At that time upwards of 170 Airacobras were in England awaiting shipment to Russia, and a decision was made to use them to equip two fighter groups for TORCH, the Russians to be compensated via the Alaska-Siberia route. The Airacobras were of the P-39D1 and P-400 vintage, types currently proving themselves inferior against the Japanese in the Solomons, and had been exposed in crates to the English weather. VIII Air Force Service Command was given the task of assembling them--it had no spare parts and no mechanics familiar with the planes-- and the 81st and 350th Fighter Groups were set up to fly them. Assembly was long delayed and the 81st Group's training with the aircraft was additionally foreshortened by adverse weather. As a result the 81st had fallen far behind the TORCH schedules when, on 27 December, 41 of its planes took off from Atcham for Port Lyautey, with the CO, Lt. Col. M. S. Wade, in the flight.

The fact that the planes were poorly assembled was revealed by the sequel. Six P-39's were interned, five in Portugal and one at Tangier; four of these were forced to land because of mechanical failure. Among the internees was Colonel Wade, and Maj. Jack Hertz temporarily assumed command of the 81st Group. On 15 January, disaster struck another P-39 mass movement when 11 more out of a flight of 61 were interned in Portugal--two landing with mechanical defects and nine because of fuel shortage brought on by bucking strong headwinds. Most of the internees were from the 350th Group. Efforts to prevent a repetition of this incident by waiting for still air or tailwinds on the route from England materially delayed the dispatch of the remaining Airacobras. The Eighth Air Force report on the subject estimates that the last got off about 1 June 1943.[18]

On the 81st's arrival in North Africa it was evidently used for a time in local defense of the Casablanca area. At Thelepte, the group was handicapped because it had no CO or staff and was forced to borrow Lt. Col. Richard P. Klocko and the staff of the 350th; moreover, according to the group, at first no one knew how to employ the P-39's. At times, they were sent out as escort for the A-20's, but finally found their most profitable occupation in "rhubarbs," that is strafing and reconnaissance missions carried out at minimum altitude with Spitfires or P-40's covering. The Airacobras flew line abreast, well spread out, each aircraft weaving. They proved remarkably resistant to the flak, but soon gave up the practice of making more than one run on a target or attacking where AA installations were known to have been provided. The 20-mm. cannon proved a reliable weapon, but the 37-mm. which was installed in the Airacobras of the 68th Observation and 350th Fighter Groups was given to jamming.[19]

Prelude to Kasserine

The Ousseltia thrust had been checked, but it had demonstrated the inability of the French to withstand German armored onslaught. AFHQ appreciated as virtual certainties that Von Arnim would launch further attacks to gain protective depth for his line of communications, and that the blows would fall on the French positions between Pichon and Faid, possibly forcing the Allies back as far as Sbeitla and Feriana. As precautionary measures General Anderson was ordered to concentrate a mobile reserve south of the First Army sector, some French units were relieved, and fresh U. S. and British troops were hurried forward as best the transportation bottleneck allowed.

XII ASC continued its assault on the enemy wherever profitable targets were discovered. On 27 January a half-dozen A-20's with P-40 escort raided the road-junction town of Lezzouna, east of Maknassy, and on the next day 12 P-40's, answering a call from the ground forces, strafed two battalions of infantry and a battery of artillery in the Ousseltia valley. Gafsa was evidently by now being used as an advanced base by XII ASC, for reports show that on the 28th a trio of Me-109's strafed it, destroying three A-20's which had landed to refuel. On the 29th two missions of a dozen escorted Bostons searched in vain for fugitive enemy truck concentrations.[30]

With the waning of the Ousseltia action, II Corps regrouped. Combat Command B was withdrawn behind Feriana to Bou Chebka, and Combat Command C—one battalion of medium tanks, one battalion of infantry, and one battalion of field artillery—moved south to reinforce Gafsa. At Sbeitla lay Combat Command A, of equal strength.

On 30 January the Germans moved again, attacking the French at Faid Pass. Employing 60 to 70 tanks, the push captured Faid by 1900 hours, but the French fell back and maintained themselves at Sidi bou Zid, a few miles to the west. Combat Command A and the 26th RCT immediately moved east from Sbeitla and other elements of the 1st

Armored were ordered to attack Maknassy from Gafsa to relieve the pressure on Faid.

XII ASC responded vigorously to the German drive. All day long its aircraft bombed and strafed in the Faid region. Four A-20 missions were flown on the 30th. At 1015 hours 11 P-40's, 6 P-39's and 6 A-20's were off against tanks in the Faid Pass. They claimed 12 out of 17 to 20 tanks left burning after the impact of 60 x 1,000-lb. bombs. The P-39's strafed and burned a half-dozen trucks, and all aircraft returned safely. Around noon, 60 more 100-pounders were dropped on a vehicle concentration, but one of the strafing P-39's was shot down and the pilot killed. Both afternoon missions were similarly successful against vehicles east of the pass.[21]

On the 31st, Combat Command A attacked the enemy positions at Faid, but the Germans had been able to get in artillery which outranged the American guns and withstood all attacks that day and succeeding ones. A good part of Colonel Williams' effort on the 31st was absorbed in defensive patrols over the ground forces at Faid and over Combat Command D attacking towards Maknassy, where eight of the 33d Group's P-40's engaged four to seven Me-109's, losing two to the enemy's one. However, the 33d, abetted by the 81st Group, took the A-20's on two offensive missions back of the enemy lines, to Bou Thadi, west of Sfax, and to the railroad east of Maknassy.

On the 1st of February, Combat Command D captured Sened Station. On the day before, it had taken a severe cuffing from the Stukas, in one instance unwisely bringing troops up to a detrucking point in vehicles ranged almost nose to tail. According to General Kuter, who spent some time studying the subject, this attack represented the only occasion when the Stukas wrought any great damage on American troops. On 1 February, probably as a result of this unhappy experience, XII ASC ran five cover missions over the area, the earliest of which caught two dozen Ju-87's escorted by Me-109's on their way in. The P-40's broke up the attack, shot down three Stukas with two probables and five damaged; two P-40's were shot down and a third listed as missing. The A-20's were also active that morning against a tank and vehicle concentration near Faid. From low level their 100-pounders scored direct hits.[22]

On the 2d, XII ASC suffered serious losses in attempting to cover the side front. The 33d Group was severely taxed to provide the umbrellas and at the same time escort the bombers of the 47th and the P-39's of the 68th Observation Group, one squadron of which had arrived at Thelepte late in January. The first cover mission, 6 P-40's and 4 P-39's, encountered 20 to 30 Stukas escorted by 8 to 10 Me-109's over Sened Station. Although one Ju-87 was destroyed, five P-40's were lost. Another reconnaissance mission of six P-40's and four P-39's which went out to the Mezzouna area met four to six FW-190's and destroyed two, but two P-40's crash-landed in enemy territory and a P-39 was reported missing. The 47th caused a large explosion in a bomb dump on one occasion and failed to find the target on another mission during which two P-40's were lost fighting off a half-dozen Me-109's.

The Germans were enjoying numerical fighter superiority over the II Corps' area and attrition was taking its toll of the 33d, XII ASC's most experienced and effective fighter unit. Replacement aircraft seem to have been available from the P-40F's of the 325th Group, which the Ranger had ferried into Casablanca, but new pilots were not available from the 325th, which was undergoing further training, or from any other source. Consequently, it was necessary to replace the 33d by a totally new organization. The 31st Group (Spitfires) began coming in to Thelepte on 6 February; earlier, two squadrons of the 52d Group had also been attached to XII ASC. The 33d went back to Morocco for rest and refitting and to pass on its experience to the 325th.[23]

Because of the failure to secure the key position at Faid Pass, Combat Command D was ordered to withdraw from Sened Station; by 4 February there remained in the southern area only one battalion of infantry at Gafsa. Combat Command B, meanwhile, had been moved to Hadjeb-el-Aioun and thence to Maktar under the mistaken impression that the enemy intended to thrust from Fondouk and Pichon into the Ousseltia valley. Defensive positions were also taken up before Faid.

On 3 February, the 321 Group went into action. It teamed with the Lafayette Escadrille to escort five A-20's on an effective attack in the Ousseltia area against a battery of 105-m. howitzers and approximately 75 trucks; somewhat later in the day it took nine more A-20's down to the region of Maknassy where frags and 100-lb. demolition bombs were dropped on tanks and motor transport. Next day the Spitfires lost two of their number and destroyed one Me-109 while on reconnaissance over Ousseltia.[34]

Part of the hard going that XII ASC was experiencing was probably due to the fact that the German squadrons facing it had been strengthened by the addition of the remains of the Desert Luftwaffe, which had run out of airfields in Libya. The Eighth Army had captured Tripoli on 23 January; by the end of the month its patrols were already over the Tunisian border. XII Bomber Command had struck at Rommel's air at the Medenine landing grounds on 24 January; and early in February, by request of Allied Air Support Command, it attempted to counter-air force action to improve the situation on XII ASC's front.[35]

The 17th Group opened the assault on 31 January, 10 of its B-26's with P-38 escort attacking Gabes airdrome with the highly effective 120-lb. frag clusters. The bursts covered the entire airdrome area, destroyed 10 parked aircraft, and put out of action a four-gun light-flak battery. The B-26's destroyed three of the Me-109's which intercepted, and the P-38's shot down two more. Two P-38's, but none of the bombers, were lost. On 2 February, the 17th was back, this time over Sfax's field in a coordinated attack with the B-25's. Fourteen of its Marauders again covered the target with bursting frags. Three of the parked aircraft were left burning, and both the B-26's and their Lightning escort got safely home. Of the 18 B-25's attacking simultaneously, one crash-landed near the target after the run through the intense heavy flak.

The treatment was continued on the 3d. Fifteen of the 17th's aircraft participated, escorted by eight P-38's from the 1st Fighter Group and eight from the 82d. Gabes was again the target--the result, 10 enemy aircraft destroyed on the ground. After the bomb run, Me-109's, which had been seen taking off from the airdrome, engaged and a 40-minute battle ensued, the Messerschmitts attacking in pairs. The B-26's claimed two destroyed, the fighters 1-2-3.* One B-26 and one P-38 crashed west of Gabes; one P-38 came down near El Guettar and another was classified as missing. Later in the day, 18 A-25's of the 310th Group struck at enemy communications back of II Corps' front with an unsuccessful attack on road and rail bridges north of Kairouan.

On 4 February the air war rose to a pitch over the Gabes fields. The B-17's made the first attacks, the 97th coming in to drop 2,592 x 20-lb. frags on the main Gabes airdrome and the 301st one minute later loosing 3,114 on a landing ground five miles to the west. Eighteen B-17's of the 97th and 12 P-38's of the 1st Fighter were over the target at 1425 in the midst of a swarm of Me-109's and FW-190's which attacked during the bomb run. The bombers claimed 9-3-6. The P-38's made no claims. The two dozen Fortresses from the 301st and their escort of 10 of the 1st Group's P-38's were likewise intercepted, the engagement turning into a 20-mile running fight in which one B-17 was shot down against bomber claims of 15-8-1 and the P-38 score of one FW-190. The frags of the combined attack destroyed 30 enemy aircraft

* One destroyed, two probables, and three damaged.

on the ground. A half-hour later, worsening weather in the area frustrated the mediums, which were briefed for a landing ground at Bordj Toual, 27 miles southwest of Gabes. The 310th's B-25's returned without incident, but 14 B-26's of the 17th Group and 10 P-38's of the 82d were attacked by enemy fighters, which shot down two of the escort.[20]

Four days later, 14 P-38's of the 82d Group escorted 18 B-26's of the 17th and 18 B-25's of the 310th on still another raid on Gabes and brought the Luftwaffe up in force. The frags covered the airdrome and the area to the north and east of it, started fires in buildings and among parked planes, and silenced two flak positions. The B-25's were severely mauled by the enemy fighters which began their attacks before the target was reached and pursued as far as the Algerian border. Although four Me-109's were destroyed by the B-25 gunners, four of the bombers were shot down and two crash-landed at base. The P-38's, meanwhile, were performing yeoman service by knocking down eight of the Messerschmitts for one P-38, and the B-26's were having their own fight with 20 to 30 Me-109's and FW-190's which attacked just after the bomb run and likewise tried conclusions all the way to the Algerian border. The B-26's destroyed six of them. On the 9th, the heavies were again briefed for the Gabes complex, but weather frustrated the 97th entirely and the 301st had to go all the way to Kairouan airdrome for a target. With 18 of the 1st Group's P-38's along, the attack was made by 24 B-17's, dropping 3,332 x 20-lb. frags on well-dispersed aircraft, two of which were assessed as destroyed. The Forts shot down one FW-190, but the P-38's had only one inconclusive encounter over Fondouk.[27]

After Combat Command D's repulse at Faid, uneasy quiet reigned for a time along II Corps' front and the French sector to the north. German tanks and motor transport began appearing on the Gabes-Gafsa road and around Maknassy. It was accepted that the Axis was about to make a last effort to disrupt the Allied timetable, the locale of the stroke anywhere from Pont du Fahs to Gafsa. Meanwhile, XII ASC flew the vital reconnaissance missions and attacked the enemy ground forces when profitable concentrations were discovered. On 8 February such a target was found 10 miles east of Faid and two A-20 missions were laid on. Six bombers, protected by 22 Spits, dropped HE and frags in a morning attack and towards evening 12 more A-20's escorted by two squadrons of Spitfires repeated the mission. The ground forces reported that four 88-mm. dual-purpose guns had been silenced, that fires had been started, and considerable equipment destroyed. On the 9th the Lafayette Escadrille bested seven FW-190's which dived from 8,000 on nine of its P-40's engaged in covering four P-39's reconnoitering near Djebel bou Dabouss. Two Focke-Wulfs were destroyed and one P-40 crash-landed near Thelepte. Two days later Sened Station was attacked by a dozen A-20's with the French squadron and one squadron of the 52d Group escorting. On the 14th the A-20's, covered by P-39's, used a mixture of HE and frag on gun installations in the same region.

Four 88's were known to have been destroyed and three more silenced.[28]

Meanwhile, the Allied Air Support Command had been developing in consonance with the command arrangements agreed upon at Casablanca. On 7 February General Kuter wired General Spaatz that AASC was exercising operational, but not administrative, control of 242 Group and XII ASC from the headquarters of the First Army at Constantine. Within a week the headquarters of the 18th Army Group, from which General Alexander would supervise the Tunisian battle, was to be set up at Constantine, and Headquarters, First Army would be going forward. General Kuter thereupon decided to send the greater part of his staff with the First Army, but he himself preferred to remain with the Army Group so that the air forces might be represented at that headquarters from the start.[29]

Communications were being established between Western Desert Air Force's advanced headquarters and AASC, and General Kuter was calling for factual data on the effectiveness of enemy air attacks on Allied troops, pointing out that "overmuch dependence has been placed on rumors and unsubstantiated reports." Other facets of "air support" were also under discussion with Allied Air Force and XII Bomber Command. "Special operations," directed against the Axis air fleets supplying Tunisia had been developed, and AASC was busy keeping abreast of the designs of AFHQ, First Army, and II Corps. On learning that an air defense wing, in addition to those at Oran and Casablanca, was being set up for Northwest Africa, General Kuter requested that it be stationed in the general vicinity of Tebessa; he estimated that an able ASC commander might double or treble the effectiveness of XII ASC's fighters. In short, Allied Air Support Command was being readied to give a good account of itself in the crisis attending the German successes at Faid and Kasserine.

Actually, the reorganization of air forces decreed at Casablanca was all but an accomplished fact. After the conference, General Spaatz had accompanied Tedder to Cairo for discussions on organization and on the necessary coordination with the Middle East. On 30 January the two airmen left Cairo, visited IX Bomber Command, picked up Air Marshal Coningham, and proceeded to Algiers on the 31st. On 1 February a B-17 of the 97th Group bore the air marshals away to England, where it was planned they would remain 10 days. By 8 February, Spaatz was writing General Arnold that the detailed studies had been accomplished and the orders prepared—to issue them he awaited only the return of Tedder.[30]

Chapter VI
XII BOMBER COMMAND--JANUARY AND FEBRUARY

The Logistic Marathon

Despite the many disappointments that the Allies had suffered in North Africa--the bitter repulse at Djedeida which condemned the armies to the cold and mud of a Tunisian winter, the enemy's spoiling attacks in the Robaa-Ousseltia sectors and at Faid Pass which had parceled out II Corps to the defense of the Eastern Dorsal--their councils entertained no doubts that in good time their armies would liquidate the Axis bridgehead in Tunisia. At Casablanca, Sir Alan Brooke, Chief of the Imperial General Staff, had even set 30 April as the probable date. Given Axis commitments elsewhere, the dominant element in this confidence was the disadvantageous Axis supply situation.

The rate and prospects of the Axis build-up seem to have been estimated somewhat differently by the strategists in Washington and London and the commanders on the spot in Africa, the differences probably a function of location and occupation. For instance, on 29 January, the Combined Intelligence Committee took an optimistic view and calculated that the practical capacity of the Tunisian ports was just sufficient to sustain a force of six German and five to six Italian divisions; of these only two German and two to three Italian divisions would be at full strength. On 6 January, on the other hand, General Eisenhower had cabled the British Chiefs of Staff: "Volume of reinforcement and supply now reaching enemy through Tunisian ports is a matter for grave concern." On 10 February, Admiral Cunningham estimated that the enemy's rate of supply and reinforcement during January and February had actually risen despite severe loss at sea.

On the Allied side, the convoys came to Casablanca, Oran, and Algiers. Both in the Atlantic and within the Mediterranean submarines stalked them, and once east of Oran each convoy had to be fought through as Bomb Alley came into operation. The most hazardous stretch of coast was from Algiers to Bone; unescorted LSI's shuttled back and forth and the convoys went up in two-week cycles. Bone itself was the Luftwaffe's favorite target; two thousand HE bombs were dropped on it from 13 December to 1 February, but, despite this hammering, 127,600 deadweight tons of cargo were discharged. Particularly heavy raids occurred early in January, the situation being improved only by laying hands on all French AA and by the dispatch of night fighters from England. At Oran and Gibraltar the Royal Navy maintained Force H, battleships and a carrier, which kept hoping that the Italian fleet would come out and which indulged in sweeps toward the Balearics and an occasional visit to Algiers. At Bone lay the aggressive Force Q, cruisers and destroyers, searching by night the Sicilian Straits.

By strictly geographical comparison, the enemy supply line was far superior. Covered by the Luftwaffe and the IAF, it led from Naples to Sicily's north coast and from Trapani and Palermo across the narrow Straits to Tunisia—contrary to a widespread impression 90 per cent of the Axis flow of men and material was seaborne, only 10 per cent airborne.

However, the Allies had already been able, by day and night bomber strikes on the ports and by naval and air action in the Straits, to inflict considerable damage. As additional Allied air power was emplaced in Africa and Malta, it was certain that the weight of these attacks would increase. If the Luftwaffe and the IAF suffered serious interim attrition, Tunisia might be cut off altogether.[1]

Whatever the future prospects, during November and December the Axis life line had been scarcely dented. After the first impact of TORCH, the enemy had passed his ships across regardless of loss; indeed he did not suffer greatly, for although British submarines had been at once concentrated in the Straits and Malta-based Albacores prowled the area by night, their efforts were mostly frustrated by weather. After the Allies were a little better established in Africa the hunting improved; the Albacores began taking toll and on the early morning of 2 December Force Q struck a convoy. The cruisers Aurora, Argonaut, and Sirius, with two destroyers, sank or fired four enemy supply ships and three enemy destroyers.

The Germans and Italians responded by giving up the night crossing. They laid minefields and crossed by day. The channel thus canalized was assailed by British submarines which did good work but soon found the going too hard. To relieve the pig-boats of the closest inshore work, British minelayers laid fields near the Cani Islands; but after drawing blood, these were soon marked by the Axis. A decision was then taken to move the submarines north of Sicily and to mine extensively the waters which they were vacating. At this juncture the

Twelfth's medium bombers took a hand; they began minimum-altitude bombing attacks in waters where enemy air power forbade Force Q's presence by day and where His Majesty's submarines had found the going generally too strong.[2]

Minimum-Altitude Attacks against Shipping

For some time the Twelfth Air Force had desired to employ the minimum-altitude technique which had been worked out at Eglin Field and had undergone successful tests and modifications in the Aleutians and Southwest Pacific. However, it had to wait upon the training of its groups and the availability of the modified N-6 gunsight and four-second-delay fuzes. As early as 11 December, P-38's had been sent on antishipping patrols off northern Tunisia, carrying one 1,000-pound bomb in place of a second belly tank. Success did not attend these ventures, although the Lightnings bombed at least one ship and had several brushes with enemy aircraft covering the convoys. The B-17's, however, were making a contribution by leaving sunken hulks here and there in the ports.

First recorded medium-bomber mission against shipping occurred on 17 December when six B-25's of the 310th Group and five B-26's of the 319th went out with an unreported number of 1st Group P-38's. No fruitful results accrued from this or two subsequent attempts, beyond stray Axis aircraft being shot down over the Straits and a number of bombed bridges in the vicinity of Tunis and Cap Bon. On 6 January, however, the day on which General Eisenhower expressed his concern over enemy reinforcement, Twelfth Air Force dispatched a radio to General Cannon: "Special counter shipping striking force will be organized immediately." The force was to consist of two to four squadrons of medium bombers, one squadron of P-38's, and a reconnaissance squadron for which Mosquitoes were being requested. Three days later, General Cannon submitted his recommendations. He objected to the formation of a special force and proposed that, instead, the countershipping function be assigned to the Bomber Command. He evidently gained his point, for at least two of XII Bomber Command's medium groups participated in shipping strikes, the escort burden being shared by all available P-38's. The reconnaissance squadron did not materialize.

During the process of setting up the antishipping force, a dispute arose as to whether it should be under the operational control of Eastern Air Command or of Twelfth Air Force. EAC based its claim on the fact that it was responsible for the reconnaissance which would provide the bombers' targets. General Doolittle, who at the time was convinced that the RAF and USAAF should be segregated as far as possible, was willing that the force be ordered out by EAC on the receipt of target information, but insisted that the Twelfth operate and service its own aircraft. It seems probable, moreover, that Cannon's recommendations were in line with his chief's efforts to retain control of his mediums.[3]

The program got underway with a very high priority around 11 January, the 310th Group (B-25's) flying most of the early sweeps, the

319th (B-26's) joining on the 15th. As many as three separate missions were flown on a single day. A typical mission consisted of a squadron of P-38's and a half-dozen B-25's or B-26's, at least that number of P-38's being needed for their own protection. The P-38's flew cover, spotting for the bombers below. Bombing was done at high speed from under 200 feet, and the 500-pounders were directed in trains of three or six at the side of the vessel. Although information on a convoy occasionally was forthcoming from intelligence or overnight reconnaissance from Malta, most of the sweeps were made "blind" in the hope of catching ships somewhere on the passage. Reconnaissance planes were not safe over the channel in daylight, as there was an oversufficiency of enemy fighters on both sides, directed by efficient radar installations. Consequently, the missions were often fruitless.[4]

For more than a week no very profitable strikes were made, but commencing 19 January the mediums began to find themselves after the overwater practice. First definite kill came on 20 January. Six B-25's of the 310th Group, escorted by 12 P-38's of the 14th Group, sighted a small merchant vessel and a 300- to 400-foot tanker, shepherded by two destroyers. One direct hit and two very near misses were scored on the tanker which underwent a violent explosion, stopped, and settled. Next day, the B-26's drew blood. Between 0940 and 1005, 15 miles west of Pantelleria, six of the 319th's bombers attacked two medium-sized freighters. They sank one and damaged the other with their bombs and strafing. The 10 accompanying P-38's had their hands full during the attack. They encountered two Cant Z-1007 bombers, which fired recognition signals: red-red-red; the P-38's shot them down but in the midst of the good work five to seven Me-109's joined from the clouds above. Two P-38's were lost, but three of the Me's were also destroyed.

On 22 and 23 January the 319th repeated its success. On the 22d, five of its B-26's attacked a small convoy in mid-channel: one freighter, one cargo liner, and two corvettes. Two hits on the freighter and near misses on the cargo liner were scored before the B-26's broke away, to be attacked by the convoy escort. Two Me-109's and two Me-110's were claimed as destroyed, and two B-26's crash-landed in the Bone area. Meanwhile the P-38's were having their own troubles with another enemy formation which included two Ju-88's, four to six Me-109's, two to four He-111's, and two unidentified four-engine aircraft. The two Ju-88's attacked, and were destroyed by the Lightnings, which lost contact with the B-26's and returned to base separately. Next day four B-26's found a freighter and a trawler in a cove near Hergla, above Sousse, and left the freighter listing. Proceeding then out to sea, the formation picked up two more freighters, exploded one, and capsized the other, while the fighters destroyed a Cant Z-1007 which flew into their formation. These results were paid for by the loss of one P-38 and one B-26.[5]

On 27 January, in mid-channel, the 310th struck two destroyers whose decks were loaded with men. A pair of direct hits and three near misses were scored on the starboard side of one of the vessels, which was last seen flaming and listing heavily. The other DD suffered probable damage to rudder and steering mechanism from the effects of four near misses. That the Axis was reacting to these attacks was evident on the same day, when seven P-38's and four B-26's sighted one large transport escorted by no less than a cruiser, two destroyers, and three corvettes, while overhead 10 to 15 Me-109's and FW-190's gave additional protection. As clouds had separated the B-26's from their escort, no attack was made. On the 29th, however, six of the 319th's B-26's performed brilliantly against a big convoy, with a dozen of the 1st Group's P-38's overhead. They picked as targets two cargo liners, out of a formation that included six freighters, four destroyers, and several smaller naval vessels. Two direct hits blew the superstructure off one of the liners. The other was fired. Sixteen enemy aircraft assailed the raiders but lost one Me-109, one Me-110, and one Me-210 to the B-26's. One B-26 crashed into the sea just after the attack, but its mates went on to explode a small vessel farther west and strafe a trawler north of Bizerte.

The antishipping sweeps went on day after day whenever weather permitted, and against them the enemy began to gather in larger convoys with abundant surface and aerial escort. Some of these concentrations were simply too strong to attack. For instance, on 31 January six B-26's and a squadron of P-38's found one ocean-going tug and two barges in company with a cruiser and two destroyers; four to eight enemy aircraft were over the convoy. The generous escort would not have turned the B-26's from their purpose, but simultaneously two large enemy air formations were observed--35 to 40 aircraft from the direction of Tunis and 40 to 50 from Bizerte. The B-26's turned for home and the P-38's followed, after destroying two Me-110's. On 2 February the 310th Group's B-25's encountered an even more formidable convoy--three merchantmen, four DD's, and a possible cruiser. Overhead, 11 enemy aircraft patrolled at 2,000 feet and 10 more at 10,000. The B-25's did not attack, but enemy aircraft engaged their escorting P-38's. One out of 15 P-38's was lost as against enemy losses of 3 Me-109's, 1 Me-110, 1 Ju-88, 1 Ju-52, and 1 Italian seaplane.[6]

On 10 February, Admiral Cunningham reviewed the progress of the war against the enemy's supply line. The Twelfth's mediums had borne heavily upon the convoys, but had not achieved the hoped-for result of forcing them to attempt the passage by night and thus present increased opportunities for the employment of Force Q. Instead, the enemy had heavily reinforced his air cover. Moreover, for lack of escort fighters and good weather, the sweeps had lately been infrequent and ineffective. This was in fact the case; no positive results had been obtained from 29 January to 9 February, but on the 10th, when the Admiral made his survey, the B-25's smashed four Siebel ferries.

The Siebel ferries are crude but useful pontoon rafts, capable, as the mediums were to discover, of mounting formidable firepower--two or three 88-mm. guns and various light AA. However, on the 10th, 9 B-25's of the 310th Group had pounced on four of them 30 to 40 miles north of Cap Bon and probably destroyed them all. One disintegrated and sank; two were left sinking and the fourth with deck awash. Men, barrels, and boxes floated away.[7]

After this strike, except for an incident on the 13th in which B-25's and P-38's collaborated to shoot down four Ju-52's and an Me-323 out of one of the huge fleets of Axis transports that daily flew the Straits, another lean period ensued. It was broken by the 310th on the 21st, when the Kasserine battle was at its height. According to the group history, the B-25's had been dispatched to head off a tanker, and 30 miles south of Sicily they found what looked to be a tanker among a convoy of several large vessels. Their 500-pounders fired the suspected tanker, sank two small escorts, and damaged a cruiser. The flak was intense and one B-25 landed in the sea. Seventeen P-38's took on the convoy's umbrella, knocked down two Ju-88's and one Italian seaplane and destroyed another Ju-88 and a Ju-52 found in the vicinity.

On the 22d, the B-25's had further success. A half-dozen of them with 10 P-38's of the 14th Group attacked two freighters escorted by three naval vessels. Despite intense and accurate light flak and the convoy's air protection, the B-25's were able to sink one of the freighters and account for an Me-109 and an FW-190, but again one of their number was lost. The P-38's claimed one Ju-88. The 310th suffered severely on the morrow when six of its aircraft made a run on 13 Siebel ferries. They sank five of the vessels, but the light flak sent three B-25's into the sea. The P-38 escort fended off all air attacks on the bombers and on the way out the Lightnings shot down one Cant Z-506.[8]

The Bomber Offensive

Despite the fact that it was shortly to become the major component of the Northwest African Strategic Air Force, XII Bomber Command could scarcely be said to be performing strategic air operations. Especially is this true if the operations of the Eighth or, later, those of the Fifteenth or the Twentieth Air Forces are considered in comparison. XII Bomber Command's overriding target was shipping--which it assailed at on- and off-loading points as well as during passage--whose cargo might reach the front and affect the battle 24 to 48 hours after tying up in any Tunisian port.

The role of cooperation in the land battle had been established from the start, when the first bombers put their wheels down on the newly-occupied African fields. On 20 January 1943, at Casablanca, the Combined Chiefs of Staff reaffirmed XII Bomber Command's preoccupation in a memorandum, "The Bomber Offensive from North Africa." In order of time the objects of Africa-based bombardment were to be: the furtherance of operations for the eviction of Axis forces from Africa; the infliction of heaviest possible losses on Axis air and naval forces in preparation for HUSKY; the direct support of HUSKY; and the destruction of the oil refineries at Ploesti. Without prejudice to any of the enumerated objectives, targets were to be chosen with a view to weakening the Italian will to war.

Having scored a tactical success in finding a means of employing its mediums against shipping--the flak had previously made their excursions to the harbors too costly--XII Bomber Command continued its efforts to interrupt the Axis supply. The B-17's were entirely satisfactory against the ports and they were kept at this work, except when higher headquarters specifically directed them to other targets. During January and February, many such directives were handed down, and the heavies frequently were to intervene directly in the land battle.[9]

The operation of 11 January was such an occasion. A small contingent of the 97th Group was sent against the fort of Gadames in Libya on a mission probably coordinated with General Le Clerc's Free French column which, having worked its way up from Fort Lamy, was operating against Italian garrisons in the Libyan interior. Five B-17's attacked, dropping 60 x 500-lb. bombs from 10,000 feet, and reported excellent results including direct hits on the fort. Photographs, however, subsequently showed the fort undamaged. Another contingent of six bombed the rail and highway bridges across the Oued El Akarit, 16 miles NNW of Gabes, and claimed two hits on the railroad bridge. The escort of 10 P-38's was unexpectedly attacked by 12 Me-109's and FW-190's and in a 25-minute battle had two of its number shot down against claims of one Messerschmitt destroyed and one probably. The bridges evidently stood, for on 15 January the 17th Bomb Group dispatched 18 B-26's which bombed them without success. Moreover, on this later occasion, the enemy sent up a dozen fighters which shot down two B-26's and two of the P-38 escort.[10]

If the heavies and mediums had no success with the Oued el Akarit bridges, they were able to hammer Rommel's air units at the Tripoli dromes, in cooperation with the advancing Eighth Army and the RAF, ME. The 319th Group inaugurated the assault on 9 January with a strike on an airfield 10 miles south of the Libyan capital, the B-26's scoring hits on hangars and an adjacent camp. On the 12th, the 97th went to Castel Benito with a mixture of frags and HE, registered hits on and in front of the hangars, and reported bursts among the parked aircraft, 20 of which were claimed destroyed. The defenders responded with light and heavy flak and 20 to 30 Me-109's, which tried to avoid the P-38's and concentrated on the bombers in a 20-minute fight. The B-17's claimed 14-3-1, one battered Fort limping in two and one-quarter hours late on two engines. Five days later, RAF, ME, signalled AFHQ that the retreating enemy had plowed and evacuated his forward airdromes and had concentrated almost 200 aircraft on Castel Benito. Middle East bombers were being turned on the target that night and a strike by the B-17's was requested for 18 January. The 97th Group performed the mission, 13 of its B-17's attacking with heavy fighter cover--33 P-38's. The bomb load was entirely HE, perhaps because the Bomber Command was suffering its perennial lack of frags; it fell on the barracks and adjacent buildings. Fifteen to 20 Me-109's and FW-190's attacked and shot down one B-17, but the bombers claimed 1-1-0 and the P-38's 2-4-4. One P-38 was missing. General Spaatz, who landed at Castel Benito late in

January on his way back from Cairo, was much impressed by the havoc wrought by the combined air efforts of Middle East and Northwest Africa.[11]

More effective than the Castel Benito strikes, in all probability, was the Bomber Command's blasting of El Aouina on 22 January. First attack was made by 26 B-17's from the 97th and 301st, escorted by 16 P-38's of the 1st Fighter. GP and frag clusters from 20,000 feet completely covered the field, with resulting fires and violent explosions, possibly because an ammunition dump had been hit. The 301st's contingent knocked down three intercepting Me-109's and all aircraft came safely back to base. About two hours later, the B-26's came over for a visit, 12 of them from the 17th Group escorted by a squadron of the 82d. They used 100-lb. bombs with 1/10 delay on the buildings along the eastern edge of the field. The last attack was carried out by 17 B-25's, escorted by delegations of eight Lightnings apiece from the 14th and 82d Groups. Their frags scored in the dispersal areas. One B-25 crashed and burned 15 miles west of Tunis, probably a victim of the flak. At least 12 parked planes were destroyed and 19 damaged by the strike--the Bomber Command's estimate was 41 destroyed--and two weeks later First Army intelligence reported that 600 Axis military casualties could be chalked up to it.[12]

The B-17's were also keeping up their "milk runs" to the ports. On 14 January the 97th went to Sousse and the 301st to Sfax. Ten Forts dropped 1,000- and 500-pounders on the Sousse docks, starting fires on the North and East quays and in the town and narrowly missing three ships in the harbor. The 301st mustered a larger force for Sfax; 24 B-17's were over the port with nine P-38's in attendance, obtaining a good concentration on the northeast jetty. In an encounter over the target two P-38's were lost and one Me-109 shot down. On 19 January Tunis sustained two attacks--the 97th striking at an industrial area south of the city and placing 85 per cent of its bombs in the target area, and the 301st scoring numerous hits on the Djebel Djelloud marshalling yards. On 20 January Tripoli harbor was the priority objective, but 13 of the 301st's B-17's found 10/10 cloud over the Libyan capital and in the haze lost contact with the 21 P-38's of the 1st Group. They thereupon proceeded without escort to Gabes and bombed Camp Mangin, destroying one of the Me-109's which rose to intercept.[13]

As new airdromes became available on the Constantine plateau, XII Bomber Command's units were gradually withdrawn from Biskra. The 301st went first--to Ain M'lila--where its air echelon arrived on 17 January. The 97th stayed on at Biskra three weeks longer, then came into Chateaudun du Rhumel. The move began on 8 February and the men at first found the cold, rain, and sleet of the plateau much less palatable than the sunny dust of Biskra. The 1st Group's P-38's followed their charges back from the desert, and after 28 January the 14th Group ceased operations at Berteaux, turned its 12 remaining P-38's over to the 82d, and settled down to await orders sending it to the rear for rest and refitting.[14]

On 23 January, the heavies returned to their favorite target--Bizerte. Eight B-17's of the 97th Group bombed shipping in the channel near the naval base and 12 of the 301st Group dropped on the base itself. Escort was by 22 P-38's of the 1st Group. The 97th sent one large merchant vessel to the bottom and damaged a second, knocked down three of 15 to 20 Me-109's which attacked during the bomb run. The 301st scored on hangars, workshops, and oil tanks, encountered 75 to 100 interceptors after the bombing run, and claimed 25 to 30 of them as destroyed.

Another of XII Bomber Command's requirements was to perform daily reconnaissance over the Gabes-Medenine-Ben Gardane road, over which Rommel's retreating forces were passing, and to attack and destroy military traffic thereon. This task fell to the P-38's, which sometimes swept the area in force. On 21 January, for instance, 24 of the 1st Group's P-38's found the road clogged with traffic, strafed until 65 vehicles were claimed as destroyed, knocked down two wandering Me-109's, and came safely back despite the fact that one P-38 had rammed a telephone pole with its wing. Next day, however, 10 Me-109's broke up another attack on the bumper-to-bumper columns by jumping eight P-38's and destroying two of them. The fight continued on the 23d over the backtracking Afrika Korps, 16 P-38's destroying 25 to 30 vehicles, but losing two of their number to a continuous engagement with the Messerschmitts. Moreover, four more P-38's did not return for unknown causes.

On the next day Bomber Command struck at the enemy air, the P-38's having reported 100 enemy aircraft on the Medenine drome. A solid overcast prevented the heavies from attacking; however, 18 B-25's of the 310th which went in under the overcast at 9,500 found the Medenine airdrome deserted but 50 to 60 aircraft on a landing ground west of the town. They dropped 1,284 frags on the target, destroying two single-engine fighters taking off. Five minutes later 18 B-26's of the 17th Group followed up in an attack with 100-pounders and destroyed one Me-109 out of a formation of interceptors. The combined assault destroyed 10 of the landing ground's parked aircraft. A little later in the day, four B-17's of the 97th struck at the shipping at Sousse, damaging a large merchantman with a direct hit.[15]

After two or three days of bad weather, the B-17's began on 28 January a series of five attacks on the ports. Sfax took its turn first. Eighteen of the 1st Group's P-38's escorted 11 B-17's of the 97th and 16 of the 301st in at 1422 to 1423 hours, the 500-pounders smashing into the docks and quays. The P-38's were inconclusively engaged by four Me-109's, but the bombers for their part knocked down four Messerschmitts. Twenty minutes later, 15 B-26's of the 17th Group rode in for another attack from 9,500 and reported large columns of smoke from the warehouse area. Their escort of eleven P-38's destroyed one out of a dozen FW-190's over the target and fought off six more enemy pursuit on the way home. The 310th Group, meanwhile, had bombed Sfax's railroad yards, 18 of the Mitchells dropping 136 x 300-pounders which scored numerous hits in the yard, on cars, and on the barracks in the near-by military camp. One P-38 was lost to flak and one B-25 crash-landed 45 miles WNW of the city, but two enemy fighters were also accounted for.

On the 29th, nine B-17's of the 97th and 13 of the 301st bored through intense heavy AA to blast Bizerte's fueling jetties and warehouses and damage one medium-sized and two large merchant vessels in the harbor. Four of the Forts sustained flak hits and a fifth crash-landed at Djebel Abiod. Next day, at Ferryville, four more vessels were damaged by a combined force from the two groups, no opposition developing other than intense flak. On the 31st at Bizerte, however, the enemy fighters came up, to lose eight of their number in an attack on a dozen of the 301st's bombers. Fourteen B-17's from the 97th, meanwhile, had bombed and sunk a large vessel at the docks. The efforts of the enemy fighters sent one B-17 into a crash landing southeast of Bone. The assault was continued on 1 February at Tunis by 10 of the 97th's Forts and an equal number from the 301st. The 97th dropped 60 x 1,000-pounders from 23,000 feet, fought off a composite attack by German and Italian pursuit for a score of 4-2-3, and had one of its Forts rammed and downed by an FW-190 apparently manned by a dead pilot. Its bombs covered the target area and damaged one large ship. The 301st attacked a convoy entering La Goulette harbor, scored one direct hit and many near misses, and shot down five Me-109's.[16]

On 7 February the Twelfth Air Force made its first attack on a target outside continental Africa—the Cagliari-Elmas airdrome in Sardinia, against which the 97th had sent 14 Fortresses as far back as November, only to have them foiled by weather. General Cannon had wanted to attack the Cagliari area for some time, as he put it, "for a diversion both for our own and enemy forces," but Twelfth Air Force had replied that Trapani and Palermo were more important objectives. However, on 6 February an Allied convoy was badly mauled between Oran and Algiers and this probably was the direct cause of the blows struck on the 7th.

A force of 51 bombers was put over the airdrome at 1508 to 1555 hours: 14 B-17's of the 97th, 18 B-17's of the 301st, and 19 B-26's of the 17th Bomb Group. The 97th attacked with 1,000-pounders, the 301st and 17th with frags. Escort for the heavies was furnished by 22 P-38's of the 1st Group, while 18 of the 82d took the mediums in three-quarters of an hour later. Results were good; bursts covered the field and hangars, destroyed 25 aircraft, and left large black-smoke fires. The 301st, attacked by eight to 10 enemy fighters, destroyed two Me-109's and damaged two Re-2001's. The 1st Fighter's contingent shot down one Me-109 on the way home, and the B-26's accounted for two more. All the Twelfth's aircraft came back to Africa, having experienced only slight and inaccurate heavy flak and having found their radio communications jammed in the target area. That evening the Allied convoy was again assailed, but weakly; and covering Beaufighters dispersed the threat.[17]

On the 8th the heavies blasted Sousse. Thirteen from the 97th and 19 from the 301st participated, escorted by two squadrons of the 1st Fighter Group. The bombing was very effective, with bursts covering the northern dock and seaplane base and causing a large explosion in the northwest corner of the harbor. Two ships took direct hits and many bombs fell among 14 to 16 small vessels. Save for an attack on Kairouan airdrome, the B-17's were then idle for a week, but on 15 February they went without escort to Palermo, kingpin of the enemy's supply route from Sicily. Eighteen of the 97th's Forts performed the mission; they left a large ship burning and reported many bombs on the docks and dry dock. No fighters rose to challenge them and the second mission to targets beyond Africa came through without loss.

Two days later, XII Bomber Command struck again at the Sardinian airdromes--the B-17's having been briefed for Elmas, the B-25's and B-26's for Villacidro. With 23 P-38's of the 1st Group escorting, the 301st had 24 of its Forts over the target at 1406 with 3,296 x 20-lb. frags and 12 x 500-lb. long fuzed, delayed-action demolition bombs. Weather prohibited observation of the results and prevented more than seven of the 97th's 20 Fortresses from bombing. The 301st destroyed one FW-190 which attacked and the P-38's, one of two Ma-200's. Forty-five minutes later the B-25's droned over Villacidro, nine of them dropping 588 x 20-lb. frags on the barracks area; the other three bombed the alternate target, Decimomannu, where they blew up a building and scored hits near parked aircraft. Four of the escorting P-38's were counted as missing, but all eventually got home. The B-26's gave up Villacidro entirely and went to Decimomannu with their frags--the bombs bursting amongst 30 to 50 parked aircraft. They shot down two Ma-200's which attacked over the target, and a Cant Z-506 was destroyed on the return trip. The only loss to bombers or escort on the mission occurred when two B-26's collided over the target--five or six chutes were observed.[18]

Attrition and the Air War

Since entering the Tunisian battle in mid-November, the Twelfth Air Force had consistently inflicted heavier losses on the GAF and IAF than it had suffered at their hands. In November it had lost only 19 aircraft to enemy air action, AA, and unknown causes but had shot down 48 enemy planes. In December the Twelfth accounted for 61 hostiles as against its own loss of 49; the box score read 167 to 72 for January and 136 to 74 for February. However, among other causes, a continuing shortage of replacement aircraft and crews hampered the TORCH air force in building this advantage into air superiority.

The TORCH plans had contemplated that, because of the difficulties of replacement, the American air units would be initially reduced to drawing replacement aircraft from their own first line strength; and General Doolittle was shortly forced to adopt this practice to fill up his active P-38 squadrons. When on 6 December, except for the advance "attrition" of the 33d Group which had been catapulted from H.M.S. *Archer* on the D-plus-5 convoy, no aircraft replacements had as yet reached the Twelfth, General Doolittle pointed out that the TORCH plans had not contemplated an early move to the east or early contact with the GAF.

The situation was not alleviated by the fact that for a variety of reasons a good portion even of the Twelfth's first-line strength had not arrived in Africa. This last-named factor was not particularly serious, however, except in the instance of the medium bombers; the Twelfth could not in any case, because of the scarcity of forward airdromes, have deployed its P-39 groups.[19]

Since the British had the responsibility of maintaining the 31st and 52d (Spitfire) Groups, and the 33d Group had not yet seen combat, the most immediate problem in early December was to get replacement B-17's, B-25's, and B-26's, and most especially, P-38's. Although B-17 combat losses were not heavy, replacements were too slow in coming to ETO; when they finally did come, the Twelfth was given priority over the Eighth—on 2 January, General Eaker explained that the "first" 28 B-17 replacements would stay in Africa.[20]

The strength of the medium groups had been cut by the 319th's bitter experience with the North Atlantic ferry route, by the use of the 310th's B-25's as navigating planes for fighters on the overwater hop from the United Kingdom, and by difficulties of range on the southern ferry route. The southern route as originally planned (Kano, Accra, or Roberts Field to Casablanca or Oran) had been based on the belief that medium bombers could negotiate a nonstop flight from the central African airdromes. However, the prevailing north winds necessitated a hurried search for intermediate fields and, finally, the moving of the overwater terminus from Accra to Bathurst. The Twelfth Air Force was scheduled to receive via this route, besides bomber replacements, the following units: 68th Observation Group (A-20 squadrons); 320th (B-26), 321st (B-25), and 17th (B-26) Medium Bombardment Groups; and the 27th Light Bombardment Group.[21]

As for the fighters, the shortage of shipping and the competition of other cargo sharply limited the two obvious methods of bringing them to Africa: by boat to United Kingdom for erection and flight to TORCH, or by boat to African ports for erection thereat. However, as the upshot of a letter from General Eisenhower to OPD, Admiral King made the Ranger available to take a load of P-40's in early January--the air echelon of the 325th Group. Moreover, at the instance of Col. Max F. Schneider, liaison officer from the Twelfth to AC/AS, Materiel, Maintenance, and Distribution, various methods of getting more fighters across were instituted by that office, the most novel of which involved the use of specially constructed steel stands for P-38's on the decks of tankers.[22]

Despite all efforts, the situation as regards P-38 replacements did not improve, and in mid-January XII Bomber Command was urgently requesting that its units be brought to strength, lest operations be curtailed. The problem came to General Arnold's attention at Casablanca and he initiated drastic action to fortify the Twelfth for the air war in the Mediterranean. On 24 January, the total strength of the three P-38 groups (less one squadron) in North Africa was 90 planes. General Arnold ordered that all P-38's in the United Kingdom be sent to North Africa immediately--the Twelfth had already scoured the United Kingdom for P-38's--and this order brought down the last of the Eighth's P-38 units, the 78th Group. Moreover, Admiral King agreed to still another crossing by the Ranger, with P-40's and replacement pilots. Additional P-38's were to be sent as deck loads and flown via the South Atlantic. General Arnold even proposed to outfit one of the Twelfth's Spitfire squadrons with P-47's, a move which was not, however, followed through. That the two Spitfire groups suffered from replacement trouble was additionally borne out by the fact that one of them, the 52d, had to be withdrawn from the Kasserine battle when that conflict was at its height; it turned its remaining aircraft over to the 31st.[33]

On 2 February General Spaatz reviewed the Twelfth's replacement status and indulged in some general remarks on serviceability in Africa. He pointed out that, in ordinary course, no more than 50 per cent of over-all aircraft strength would be serviceable for operations and that therefore to keep at strength an active combat unit, at least 50 per cent additional strength above T/O must be available in the theater. He indicated that the low number of B-17's then in operation was due rather to motor changes caused by sand, i.e., at Biskra, than to any shortage of aircraft. However, on the 20th he was complaining of a "critical" situation in his medium and light bombardment units, and not until 26 March was he able to write of a "very, very noticeable improvement" in replacement aircraft.[24]

Replacement pilots were no more plentiful than aircraft during the early phases of the Tunisian battle and the consequent lowering of morale in the affected units was cited time after time in the pleas to

Washington for reinforcement. The policy of the "full breakfast table" could not be maintained. In the review of his replacement situation which Spaatz made on 2 February, he emphasized the need for a replacement pool for the rapid dispatch of pilots to meet losses from combat. The upshot of the twin scarcities was that the Twelfth was forced to the uneconomical practice of relieving entire squadrons and groups, often under the least convenient circumstances. The case of the 52d Group has already been cited; the replacement of the 15th Light Bombardment Squadron early in January and of the 33d Group in the first week of February deprived XII ASC of two experienced and effective units, and the latter's relief came in the midst of intensive air operations. Similarly, in the Bomber Command, the 319th Medium and 14th Fighter Groups were retired during the month of February.[25]

The shortage of fighter aircraft in the Twelfth Air Force was the more serious in that all echelons agreed that numerical superiority was necessary for success against the FW-190 and the Me-109G1 and G2. At no time did Bomber, Fighter, or Air Support Command consistently enjoy over the enemy a preponderance of fighter strength. Bomber Command recognized two distinct types of escort--depending upon the numerical ratio of fighters to their charges. When the ratio was low--and it generally was--close escort was not attempted. The fighters made an offensive sweep of the area ahead of the bomber formation and retired following the last group of bombers.

As to the record of the P-38 against the GAF's fighters, a certain amount of disagreement exists and cannot be reconciled in the absence of fighter-versus-fighter statistics. Admittedly, in escort work the P-38's suffered from the inherent handicap of a defensive role in which they were obliged to await attack under conditions chosen by the enemy, but it is probable that they held their own even under this circumstance and their chances improved when they were used independently. Their pilots had no inferiority complex, the bomber crews regarded them as indispensable, and the Twelfth Air Force never ceased calling for them, making no complaint of their performance.[26]

The tropicalized Spitfire V, with which the 31st and 52d U. S. Fighter Groups were equipped, as were most of Eastern Air Command's fighter squadrons, did not measure up to either the FW-190 or the Me-109G2. On 12 January General Eisenhower dispatched a personal message to Sir Charles Portal in reference particularly to the air war over Bone. He spoke of the "severe tactical handicap" under which Spit V pilots labored, and in order to score a tactical surprise on the GAF, asked that two or three RAF squadrons, instead of the one squadron presently contemplated, be equipped with Spit IX's. XII ASC's comment on the Spit V, as well as the P-40F, was that it was necessary to employ large formations because the speed and climb of the enemy aircraft enabled them to choose whether to attack or run.

The P-40F, at altitudes under 12,000 feet, could be used successfully against any of the Axis fighters, but as the Lafayette Escadrille discovered, it could not dogfight above 12,000 nor climb into the sun against them. On 4 February AFHQ requested that when the Ranger again loaded P-40's for Africa they be of the P-40N variety as "earlier P-40 types are badly handicapped in fighting latest Axis equipment." As for the P-39D1's and P-400's they simply did not have the fighter characteristics the theater required.[27]

Performance of the Mediums

The Twelfth's heavy bombers--two experienced groups--had turned in generally excellent performances. Their bombing accuracy was good, from an altitude where losses from flak were low, and their gunners accumulated formidable claims against enemy interceptors. The tactical value of the medium bombers, however, at times seemed to approach the equivocal. At low altitudes (4,000 to 6,000 feet) light flak made their excursions expensive; at 9,000 to 12,000 feet their bombing accuracy did not justify the adjective "precision," and at any altitude they were more difficult to escort and, especially the B-25's, more vulnerable to enemy fighters. Their main advantage over the heavies lay in the fact that they could be dispatched more quickly against any target, an important consideration when enemy convoys were reported in the Straits. The Straits had been the scene of their main successes in January and February, but even there they had begun to encounter effective enemy countermeasures. Moreover, the B-25 and B-26 squadrons suffered considerably in morale and effectiveness because of the failure to keep them at strength.[28]

During January, the medium groups made a series of attacks on railroad targets which affords a fair sampling of their general bombing performance. On the 10th, nine B-26's of the 17th Group were briefed for an attack upon a column of tanks reported on a road west of Gabes. Unable to find the Panzers, they made a run on the marshalling yards and oil tanks at Gabes itself, with 192 x 100-lb. demolition bombs and 19 x 100-lb. incendiaries. Results from 8,000 to 8,500 feet were excellent with a direct hit on an oil tank and the destruction of large sections of track. Two Me-109's attacked the escort of 8 P-38's, one Lightning subsequently being reported missing, and an assault by four to six He-109's shot down one of the bombers against bomber claims of 1-1-0. On the 14th the railroad yards and warehouses at the little seaside town of Mahares were the targets for a half-dozen of the 319th's Marauders. Of the 50 x 300-lb. bombs, only one was claimed to have hit the railroad and two in the neighborhood of the warehouses. One string, however, hit a group of boats offshore. Better results had been obtained two days before on the bridges at La Hencha by 12 B-26's from the 17th. Attacking from 5,000 to 7,500 feet they blew up the road bridge and scored near misses on the railroad bridge. Not content, the formation continued to Chebba and obtained two hits on a bridge at that place.[29]

As frequently happened in Africa, dust obscured the results of a strike at the railroad junction of Graiba on 17 January. The 12 B-25's of the 310th Group could only report one stick in the southwest portion of the target area. On the 30th, however, the B-25's not only registered effectively on railroad installations at El Aouinet, but brought the local Luftwaffe up for a minor air battle. On that day 18 Mitchells went out with 15 P-38's of the 82d Group. They bombed from 8,200 to 9,600, put one string across the tracks, placed others on the main track and spurs, and reported bursts in the warehouse area. Just after the run 10 to 12 Me-109's and 3 to 4 FW-190's appeared. The bombers claimed 2-2-0, the P-38's five Messerschmitts and a Focke-Wulf destroyed. Two P-38's crashed north of Gabes and two were listed as missing.

The mediums usually proved quite successful against airdromes. On 29 January both the 17th and the 310th dispatched contingents against El Aouina. The B-25's, approaching from the landward side, were confronted by 10/10 overcast and did not bomb, but 11 B-26's came in from the sea and dropped 1,152 x 20-lb. frags--the bursts covering the airdrome, demolishing the buildings on its east side. A direct hit put out a flak position and 12 enemy aircraft were destroyed on the ground. A dozen enemy fighters made interception: the B-26's shot down three, their escort destroyed one, and the 310th's escort, observing the fight over Mateur, lent a hand by knocking down still another. On 13 February the B-26's did not fare so well over El Aouina. Twenty-five of them from the 17th and 319th started for the target, but twelve returned early, probably because of the bad weather. Seven-tenths overcast shrouded the Tunis airdrome, with broken clouds at 12,000 feet, and only partial observation of the results of the frags could be made. The bombers had meanwhile lost their escort in the clouds and found themselves the target, not only for 15 minutes of intense flak but for 20 to 30 Me-109's. Bomber claims ran to 4-3-4; one B-26 crash-landed in friendly territory with a dead crew member, and another bomber had gone down over the target.[30]

In the first days of February, the Twelfth's mediums received reinforcements—the 81st and 82d Squadrons of the 12th Group (B-25's), which had earned a formidable reputation in the Ninth Air Force. The orders were received at Gambut on 2 February, and in the succeeding days the air echelon and part of the ground echelon of the two squadrons departed for Biskra in Algeria. They subsequently moved to Berteaux, in time to take a hand, as did almost every combat echelon of the Twelfth Air Force, in the discomfiture of the Axis before Thala and Tebessa.[31]

Chapter VII
THE TURN OF THE TIDE

The Axis Break-Through

By mid-February the Axis held in central Tunisia the most favorable position it could expect for the duration of the campaign. The Eighth Army was walled off beyond the Mareth fortifications, under the necessity of building up supplies through Tripoli and additionally hampered by bad weather. In the breathing spell before General Montgomery could mount an attack on the Mareth Line, there was scope for an adventure against the ill-equipped French on the Eastern Dorsal and the largely untried American II Corps which had assembled forward of Tebessa in January. The 21st Panzer Division, withdrawn from the Afrika Korps and partially re-equipped at Sfax, had already put in an appearance at Faid Pass on the 30th of January, and on 12 February Rommel detached additional armor and sent it northward through the Gabes gap.

On 14 February, in strict accordance with Rommel's "Appreciation," the enemy launched an attack designed to cut through both the Eastern and the Western Dorsal, take Le Kef, and from there roll on to the coast, isolating the Allied forces facing Tunis and Bizerte. At the very least, the move would serve to safeguard the Axis flank during the Eighth Army's inevitable smash at the Mareth Line. The chief point of assault was Sidi Bou Zid, a subsidiary attack developing from Maknassy.

The defense of Sidi Bou Zid was the responsibility of the U. S. 1st Armored Division and rested on two hill positions facing Faid Pass and a mobile reserve in Sidi Bou Zid itself. According to II Corps' report the hill positions were not mutually supporting for antitank and small-arms fire. By nightfall the enemy had overrun two batteries of American field artillery, inflicted heavy losses on counterattacking American armor, and completely cut off the infantry on Djebel Lessouda.

XII Air Support Command immediately threw itself into the battle. On the 14th its fighters carried out repeated reconnaissance and strafing missions, and the A-20's bruised a tank column in Faid Pass with demolition and frags. During this attack, the escort became involved with an unreported number of FW-190's which engaged the close cover of P-39's and P-40's. Spitfires, flying top cover, dived to attack but found their guns had been jammed by a sand storm. However, the P-39's and P-40's destroyed one FW-190 without loss to themselves. The A-20's also participated in three missions against the southern horn of the enemy's advance, the most notable of which caught a convoy of perhaps a hundred trucks at an undispersed halt northwest of Maknassy. Moreover, on the way to the target the escort broke up a fighter-bomber raid of Me-109's and FW-190's.

In view of the menacing situation at Sidi Bou Zid the small garrison of French and Americans at Gafsa withdrew to Feriana on the

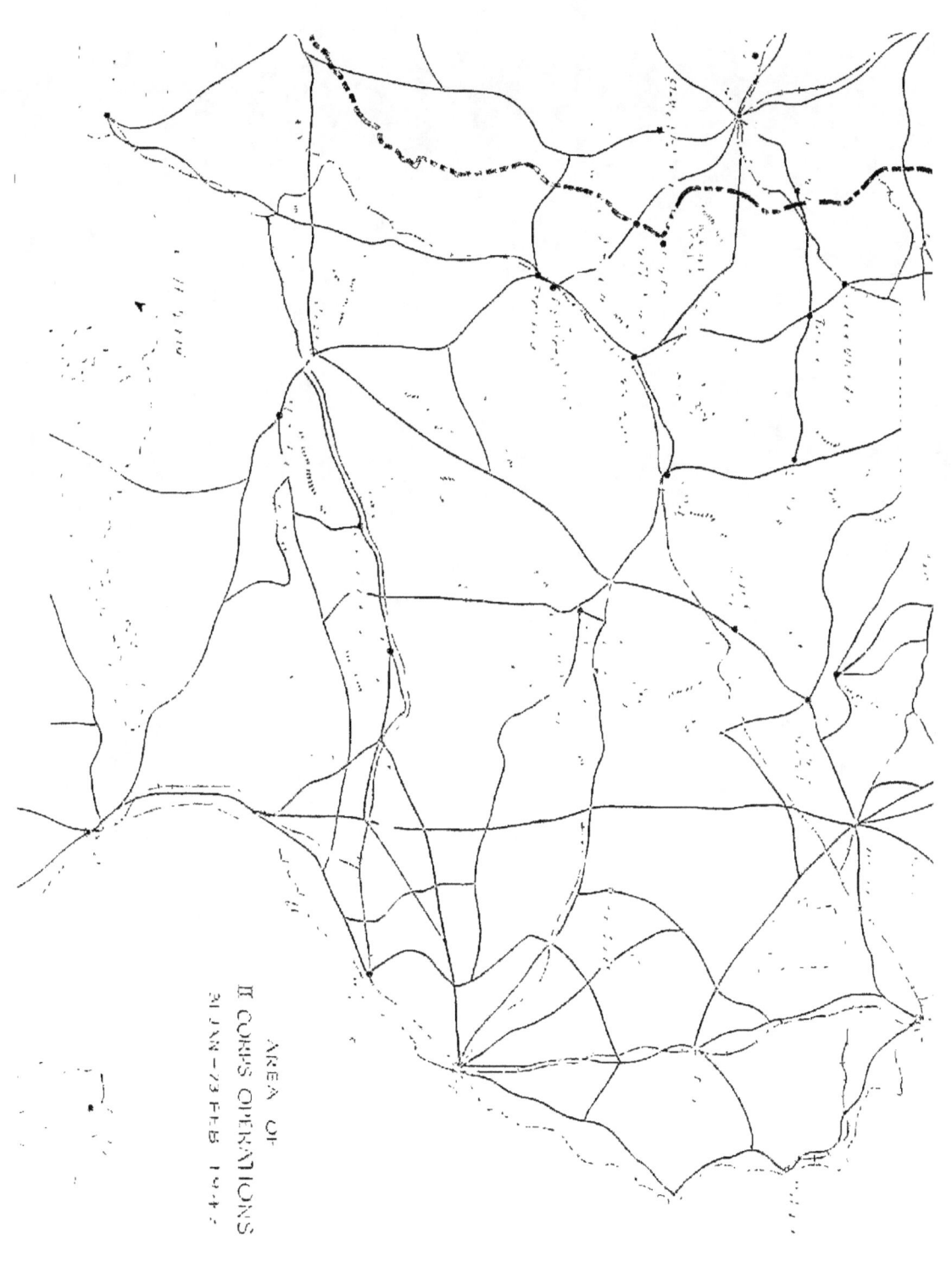

AREA OF
II CORPS OPERATIONS
21 JAN-13 FEB 1943

night of the 14th. The next morning, the 1st Armored attempted to relieve the 168th Infantry still holding Djebels Lessouda and Ksaira. Despite heavy sacrifices in tanks, the action did not succeed in extricating the infantry, although some of Djebel Lessouda's defenders managed to escape during the night, the orders to retire having been dropped by two P-39's of the 81st Group. Contact was lost with the troops on Djebel Ksaira and with the 2d Battalion, 1st Armored Regiment, which had reached the outskirts of Sidi Bou Zid during the counterattack.

On the 15th, XII ASC's principal efforts went to the protection of the embattled line. The day at Thelepte began with a strafing attack by six Me-109's, necessitating the recall of the first mission. Twelve Spitfires and two P-39's, of the 31st and 81st Groups respectively, returned in time to destroy three of the raiders. One Spit was downed, and an A-20 was strafed and destroyed on the ground. All day the Spits and P-39's patrolled and strafed in the region of Sidi Bou Zid. On the 14th XII ASC's reconnaissance had revealed Kairouan field well stocked with enemy aircraft, and General Kuter at AASC had accordingly requested a strike by XII Bomber Command. General Spaatz having set up medium bombers for XII ASC's needs on the 15th, the attack was carried out on that day by the newly arrived squadrons of the 12th Group and the B-26's of the 17th. Thirteen B-26's hit Kairouan first, the frags catching two aircraft taking off. Nine of the 12th's B-25's followed in a half-hour; as they came in on the target they could see three enemy aircraft afire, the fruits of the previous attack. Although intense light and heavy flak greeted them, they laid their frags on the sides of the runways and on the dispersal areas. Both formations were intercepted, but the bombers and escort compiled claims of seven enemy fighters destroyed against one B-25 hit by flak and then shot down.

February 16th saw Combat Command A in a delaying action east and southeast of Sbeitla, suffering heavy personnel casualties from dive bombing. It was by now apparent that the whole area east of the Western Dorsal was untenable, as II Corps' losses of 98 medium tanks, 57 half-tracks, 12 x 155-mm. and 17 x 105-mm. guns rendered counterstrokes impossible. XII ASC did its utmost in the deteriorating situation, its fighters furnishing cover and its light bombers attacking trucks, tanks, and gun positions. However, Gafsa had already on the night of the 15th been occupied by a small enemy column, and the orders had gone out to organize Kasserine Pass for defense. As a result XII ASC was forced to evacuate most of its airdromes.1

During the week of 14-21 February, XII ASC successively evacuated five bases in the path of the enemy onslaught, simultaneously maintaining a high level of air activity as its contribution to a critical situation. This achievement redounded to the credit not only of the individual Air Corps units involved but to the careful advance planning of Allied Air Support Command. The possibility of "retrograde movement" in II Corps' area had figured in headquarters calculations for some time prior to 14 February, and on 10 February Evacuation Plan A for

Sbeitla and Thelepte had been disseminated to the interested commands.

As measures preliminary to the invocation of Plan A, stockage at the Thelepte dromes was to be immediately reduced to a four-day level for units presently located there; and Sbeitla, where no tactical units had arrived, was not to receive stockage in excess of a four-day level for one fighter group. A further precaution was the build-up at Canrobert of a 10-day stockage for one light bomb group. Once Plan A was declared in effect, the units occupying Sbeitla and Thelepte were to be moved to Youks, Tebessa, and Le Kouif as determined by XII ASC, and stockage at Thelepte was to be reduced to a four-day level for one fighter group. The 3d Service Area Command became responsible for the removal of supplies and equipment from Sbeitla and Thelepte. XII ASC was to assist this process to the maximum, determine the priorities for movement of supplies and personnel, and destroy equipment and stores likely to fall into enemy hands.

Plan A was to go into operation if and when the ground forces withdrew from Gafsa. When this event occurred on the evening of the 14th, Plan A was declared in effect as of 2200 hours--but for Sbeitla only, the time of its application to the Thelepte dromes being left to the XII ASC commander, Colonel Williams. During the night of 14-15 February, Sbeitla was accordingly abandoned and the resident 46th Service Squadron departed for Canrobert.

General Kuter had previously intended to base the 68th Observation Group at Sbeitla, and the station had been occupied by Service Command troops since 1 February. However, the uncertain ground situation had given the AASC commander pause. The 46th Service Squadron was working at Sbeitla when the evacuation orders came; it was very nearly captured by the oncoming Axis forces, but escaped and took with it 75 truck-loads of supplies, a three-day level of munitions, and more than 100,000 gallons of gas and oil.[2]

The valuable Thelepte fields were given up by the 17th, as the Allied line was swung back on the Western Dorsal and the Germans and Italians approached from Gafsa and Sbeitla. Two A-20 squadrons of the 47th Group were ordered out first. On the 16th the ground personnel began preparing the evacuation while the aircrews were on a mission. By 2400 of the 16th, the two squadrons had joined the rest of the group at Youks-les-Bains where daylight of the 17th found them ready for action. Thelepte's two fighter groups, the 31st and the 81st, followed on the 17th, the last personnel pulling out as Axis artillery began registering on the airdromes. The 81st went back to Le Kouif, northwest of Tebessa, and the 31st to a makeshift field at Tebessa itself. Also directed to Le Kouif was the 346th Squadron of the 350th Fighter Group.

From the two Thelepte fields, a total of 3,496 individuals were evacuated and very little organizational equipment was left behind. Fifty thousand gallons of gasoline were burned as well as four P-40's, three A-20's, three Spits and eight P-39's; of these, five were non-reparable. On 18 February, instructions were issued from AASC that neither gasoline nor aircraft were to be burned in any further evacuations;

rather the gasoline containers were to be punctured and the planes disabled only to the extent of rendering their use by the enemy impossible.

Intensive air operations continued. On the 17th the Spits and P-39's performed their reconnaissance missions over the fluid front, strafed where targets presented themselves, and furnished cover for Combat Command A stubbornly defending Sbeitla. A Spitfire squadron up at 1115 hours reported one of the Thelepte fields being shelled and Feriana swarming with Axis transport. Late in the afternoon six A-20's struck the road below Feriana, claiming 35 vehicles destroyed after a low-altitude attack with 100-lb. bombs fuzed for delayed action. A road and a highway bridge were also declared out. One A-20 and one Spit were lost to flak.[3]

The Crisis before Thala

By 18 February, II Corps had pulled back into the Western Dorsal and was busily fortifying the passes in the barrier: Sbiba, El-Ma-El-Abiod, Dernaia, and Kasserine. Everywhere on the hills guns were being emplaced and foxholes dug. The remains of Combat Command A moved from Sbeitla into the Sbiba gap where it was joined by elements of the British 6th Armored. To watch over El-Ma-El-Abiod, Combat Command B moved to the region southeast of Tebessa, while Djebel Dernaia's three approaches were organized for defense by the former Gafsa garrison. The tactical importance of Kasserine Pass lay in the fact that meeting in the defile were two roads, leading northwest to Thala and west to

Tebessa--and except at the fork, communication between them was impracticable because the Oued Hateb was in flood. Consequently, not only was the Pass itself fortified, but the 26th Infantry dug in along the Thala road and the 19th Engineer Regiment went into position blocking the Tebessa route.

On 18 February, in the midst of II Corps' travail, General Spaatz issued his GO #1, activating the Northwest African Air Forces. The previous day had witnessed Air Marshal Coningham's arrival at 18th Army Group and his assumption of command over AASC, which, pursuant to GO #1, became Northwest African Tactical Air Force. The air marshal made himself felt at once. Upon perusing the operations summary for the 18th, he was moved to cable all air commands deploring the fact that almost all flying done by XII ASC and 242 Group had been defensive. Targets were in evidence; bombers were on call, but had not been utilized, nor had fighters been used offensively. Coningham informed his air commanders that he had already advised the 1st Army and the three corps headquarters that cover flying was being abandoned unless specifically authorized by NATAF. Hereafter, the maximum offensive role was to be assigned to every mission. The air marshal pointed out that by going on the offensive the air force automatically protected the ground forces. Moreover, he indicated that in the present critical phase of operations, every opportunity should be taken to strike at enemy concentrations and soft-skinned vehicles--tanks were to be let alone.[4]

XII ASC's activity during the worsening weather of 18 February had consisted of four missions--two reconnaissance and strafing missions at Sbeitla and Feriana and two troop-cover missions in the Kasserine area, where the enemy was probing the defenses of the Pass. The day of the 19th allowed no scope for flying, offensive or defensive, as drenching rains set in. The 20th proved little better. While XII ASC sat waterbound, the Germans and Italians put their time to good advantage. The defenses of Sbiba resisted all attacks, but on the night of the 19th the enemy infiltrated the high ground overlooking the American positions at Kasserine Pass. At daylight he attacked and broke through.

By now energetic measures had been taken to meet the deepening crisis. The British 26th Armored Brigade had come under II Corps' control near Thala on the 19th and additional reinforcements were on the way. By the 20th General Spaatz had placed most of his Strategic Air Force (XII Bomber Command plus two Wellington squadrons) at Air Marshal Coningham's disposal. This arrangement obtained throughout the critical phase of the operations and was still in force on 24 February. The stage was being set for a concentration of air power which was to go far to blunt the Axis spearheads.

In the face of the enemy onslaught, the 26th Infantry had been forced to retire up the Thala road, compelling in turn the withdrawal of the 19th Engineers on its side of the Oued Hateb. Combat Command B, moving to the support of the engineers, went into defensive positions eight miles east of Djebel Hamra and the 26th Armored Brigade prepared to dispute an advance on Thala. On the night of the 20th, General

Robinett and the British commanders agreed on a plan to halt the enemy push. General Robinett was to restore the situation south of the Oued Hateb while the 26th Armored Brigade was to fight a delaying action to enable the 2d Battalion, 5th Leicesters, to prepare positions across the road three miles from Thala. It was up the Thala road that the enemy was making his main effort, and it was imperative that he not reach the Leicesters before 1800, 21 February.[5]

The day of 21 February compassed a desperate struggle. The Axis forces debouched from Kasserine Pass, hit towards Tebessa with 20 tanks and towards Thala with 40. Combat Command B contained all thrusts towards Tebessa, but the 26th Armored Brigade lost 20 tanks in the day's action. The brigade maintained, however, the required delay. When at 1945 the enemy broke the Leicesters' position before Thala, he was confronted by the artillery of the U. S. 9th Division, which had spent four days and nights in a hasty journey from Casablanca. Orders were circulated that the position must be held at all costs.

Again on the 21st, weather hampered XII ASC's efforts to intervene in the battle. On four occasions its Spits and P-39's rose on reconnaissance and strafing missions; three times they were forced back by rain and fog. Only two P-39's were able to bore through to the enemy, strafing a concentration of 20 tanks and 20 to 40 trucks. Strategic Air Force contributed a raid on the Gafsa railroad yards by 10 B-25's of the 12th Group. On this day also, XII ASC's units evacuated another field, Tebessa, the 31st Fighter Group's 307th and 309th Squadrons going back to Youks and the 308th to Le Kouif. Le Kouif, in turn, was abandoned on the 22d, with the 308th Squadron and the entire 81st Group landing again at Youks.

February 22d was the critical day. The Axis tide reached its flood. It beat against Sbiba where two newly arrived squadrons of Churchill tanks bested the Panzers in their first engagement. It lapped at the defenses of Thala and Tebessa--without, however, breaching them. At 1915 the enemy began a general withdrawal, hastened by a successful American counterattack which cleared him out of Bou Dries. All night the Allied artillery harassed his movements with interdiction fire.

Thanks to partially clearing skies, the air forces were able to contribute to the final repulse, with XII ASC bearing the brunt. Youks-les-Bains, the Twelfth's first advanced base in Africa, had become the focus of air activity by the 22d. Despite the fact that Air Corps troops not needed for immediate operations had been previously sent back to Canrobert, Youks was a badly crowded field, entertaining echelons of various strength from the 47th Light Bombardment, the 31st, 81st, and 33d Fighter Groups, the 154th Observation Squadron, and the Lafayette Escadrille, in addition to Service Command personnel. Day and night, an ominous procession of evacuated troops and material passed by the field on the way to the comparative safety of Ain Beida and Constantine. Operations proceeded from one steel runway, on which, as Youks was the only available forward base, transports and courier planes were constantly landing and taking off, posing a formidable problem of traffic control. Tactical squadrons lent a hand to the harassed and overworked Service Command complement in this and other matters.

During most of the crucial 22d, Youks was out of communication with Headquarters, XII ASC, which was being prepared for evacuation. However, operational policy had been established by a radio message from Colonel Williams that was received at the airfield on the night of the 21st. All possible aircraft were to be put over the Thala area on the morrow, and a schedule of continuous missions was drawn up for a dawn-to-dark assault on the enemy. Actually, the command was able to lay on the creditable total of 23 missions, 114 sorties.

The 22d dawned as had its predecessors with intermittent showers and a low ceiling. Not until midmorning did the skies relent enough to permit the first of ten A-20 missions to set off at 1135. Down at Kasserine Pass, low clouds over the flanking 5,000-foot hills added navigational dangers to the strikes, many of which were carried out by pairs of unescorted Bostons. Results could not accurately be determined in the low visibility, but one effective attack brought a congratulatory message from Air Support Control. In accordance with instructions from AASC, Lt. Col. Fred M. Dean, CO of the 31st Fighter Group, had been given supervision of all the fighters at Youks, and his P-39's and Spits continually took off on strafing, reconnaissance, and escort missions. Although the flak still spat at the low-flying

American planes, the Luftwaffe was comparatively ineffective in the crisis. Aircraft losses were light. One A-20 crash-landed after an encounter with three Me-109's over the Pass, but Spitfires disposed of a Ju-88 and a Stuka during the day.

The spotty weather prevented full employment of Strategic's power. Of five bombing missions dispatched, three brought back their bombs, and of 22 B-17's of the 97th Group over Kasserine Pass at 13,000 feet, only seven dropped their frags. A dozen B-25's of the 12th Bomb Group, which rendezvoused over Youks with two Spitfire squadrons, attacked a bridge near Kasserine with unobserved results. The strafing work of XII ASC's P-39's was supplemented by Strategic's P-38's, two squadrons of which worked over the traffic moving through the Pass.[6]

Next day all efforts were bent to punishing the enemy in his retreat through the Kasserine defile. The planes flew out continuously from Youks, and in the evening 155-mm. began registering on the Pass. XII ASC performed 10 missions, 131 sorties, in indifferent weather. Four A-20's which attacked an Axis vehicle concentration southeast of Kasserine reported 10 single-engine aircraft on one of the Thelepte fields--it was known that the Germans were using the Thelepte bases. Another A-20 strike destroyed at least eight vehicles on the Feriana-Kasserine road. Probably the most successful mission was carried out by six P-39's of the 81st Fighter Group which, covered by a Spitfire squadron, caught another column on the same road and shot up 20 vehicles including trucks laden with troops.

The heavy bomb groups flew both morning and afternoon missions on the 23d, the morning missions being directed against Axis airfields. Twenty B-17's of the 97th, off at 0800, found Gabes West landing ground cloud-shrouded, but the 301st's contingent of 24 Forts covered Kairouan airfield with their frags. In the afternoon, the heavies returned--the 97th, unescorted, to lay frags on the stretch of road between Kasserine town and the Pass, and the 301st to attack the town through holes in the clouds. Meanwhile, two formations of mediums had been dispatched against enemy positions in the Pass. Seventeen B-26's of the 17th Group scored on gun positions, losing one bomber to the AA. B-25's of the 12th Group had earlier been over the Pass, but the overcast caused them to go on in the direction of Sbeitla and bomb the heavy traffic streaming towards Faid.

In the days following 23 February, the Germans and Italians continued to fall back--their armor urgently needed in the south to stem the Eighth Army's imminent blow at the Mareth system. Hereafter the Allies were almost continuously on the offensive in Tunisia, although Von Arnim shortly mounted an "opportunist" push in the Mateur-Sedjenane sector, on the theory that the southward flow of reinforcements to II Corps would have weakened the northern sector, and early in March Rommel pushed a spoiling attack at the Eighth Army which fizzled out in the face of the British artillery. The air phase of the Kasserine battles had given unmistakable signs of fruitful

Allied cooperation under NAAF's aegis. The former Eastern Air Command had contributed Hurribomber squadrons to the enemy's discomfiture before Thala, and nightly the Bisleys had bombed the key highways through the Dorsals. Western Desert Air Force, for its part, had attacked and pinned down the GAF in southern Tunisia. A new era in the African air war was beginning.[7]

The Northwest African Air Forces

February 1943 witnessed the marrying of the Middle East and Northwest African theaters of war. General procedures for the union had been laid down the month before at Casablanca, in preparation for HUSKY, and AFHQ had been working out the details. On 20 February, General Eisenhower announced sweeping command changes in his ground and sea arms. General Alexander became Deputy Commander in Chief, Allied Force and commander of the 18th Army Group, comprising the British First and Eighth Armies and the XIX French and II American Corps. Fleet Admiral Sir Andrew Cunningham succeeded Adm. Sir Henry Harwood as Commander in Chief, Mediterranean; and Malta passed out of the Middle East command, although it could not yet be supplied through the Sicilian narrows.[8]

The parallel integration of the air forces was entrusted to the Mediterranean Air Command, constituted and activated by AFHQ on 17 February, pursuant to a CCS directive of 20 January 1943. Air Chief Marshal Tedder was named commander. MAC became responsible for cooperation with the Allied armies in Tunisia, for the training and replacement of RAF and USAAF personnel, for the supply and maintenance of the combined air forces, and for the protection of Allied shipping, ports, and base areas. Its counter-air force activities were intended to forward the Tunisian battle, strip the aerial resources of Sicily, and divert GAF strength from the summer campaign in Russia. Its strategic bombing effort, directed against Axis land, sea, and air communications, had the objects of isolating the Tunisian bridgehead and interrupting any build-up of the Sicilian defenses. For operations in Northwest Africa, MAC was subordinate to AFHQ.

Air Marshal Tedder brought to these tasks a formidable air power. He disposed of the U. S. Ninth and Twelfth Air Forces; the RAF Eastern Air Command; RAF, Middle East; and RAF, Malta; he was also invested with operational control of RAF, Gibraltar. His headquarters, which was to be a small policy and planning staff--as one commentator put it, "a brain trust without executive authority or domestic responsibilities"--commenced activity on 18 February at Algiers, in the building occupied by AFHQ. Among the personnel brought from Air Marshal Tedder's old Cairo offices were Air Vice Marshal H. E. P. Wigglesworth, who became his Deputy, and Air Vice Marshal C. G. Dawson, who filled the post of Director of Maintenance and Supply. General Craig, formerly CG, XII ASC, was appointed Chief of Staff for MAC and Brig. Gen. P. W. Timberlake became Director of Operations and Plans.[9]

The administrative functions of MAC were performed by its three subordinate commands: Northwest African Air Forces, General Spaatz commanding; Middle East Air Command, Air Marshal Douglas commanding; and RAF Malta Air Command under Air Vice Marshal Sir Keith Park. Of these the chief component was Northwest African Air Forces.

The genesis of NAAF can be traced from the negotiations attending the establishment of Allied Air Force early in January 1943 through the Casablanca conference, at which the essential features of the command were laid down. Details of the organization had been thrashed out by a committee which Allied Air Force set up under General Craig's chairmanship on 3 February. Allied Air Force itself was abolished by the AFHQ order which set up MAC and its personnel, units, and establishments were transferred to MAAF.

By the terms of the reorganization, Malta had passed under the direct command of MAC. Otherwise no significant change of function or organization occurred in the Malta or Middle East commands. As for NAAF, to it was sublet as much of the functions of MAC as could be performed from the NAAF base area and with the NAAF resources: neutralization of enemy air forces; cooperation with the Tunisian land battle; interruption of the enemy's sea, land, and air communications with Northwest Africa. In addition, Allied shipping, ports, and back areas were to be protected, a central organization for supply of USAAF and RAF units set up, and training and replacement provided for.

Initially, NAAF involved the combining of Eastern Air Command and the Twelfth Air Force. Activation day was 18 February, and from the shuffling of RAF and USAAF elements five new subcommands emerged: Northwest African Tactical Air Force, Northwest African Strategic Air Force, Northwest African Coastal Air Force, Northwest African Training Command, and Northwest African Air Service Command. On 21 February, operational control of Western Desert Air Force passed to General Spaatz, to be exercised by the Tactical Air Force.

Northwest African Tactical Air Force, under the command of Air Marshal Coningham, was charged with cooperation with the Allied ground forces converging on the Tunisian bridgehead: 242 Group (Air Commodore K. B. B. Cross) to cooperate with First Army, XII ASC (Colonel Williams) to cooperate with II Corps, and Western Desert Air Force (Air Vice Marshal Harry Broadhurst) to cooperate with Eighth Army. Air Marshal Coningham moved his headquarters to the Souk el Khemis area near General Alexander's advance 18th Army Group headquarters and General Anderson's First Army battle headquarters.

General Doolittle took over the Strategic Air Force, composed of XII Bomber Command and two British Wellington squadrons, based generally on a group of airdromes around Constantine, where Headquarters, NASAF was set up. The Coastal Air Force was given the responsibility for air defense of North Africa, sea/air reconnaissance, antisubmarine air operations, air protection of shipping, and the carrying out of strikes against enemy shipping. It comprised Headquarters and Headquarters Squadron, XII Fighter Command; 1st and 2d Air Defense Wings; the U. S. 350th Fighter Group; and 323, 325, and 328 Wings,

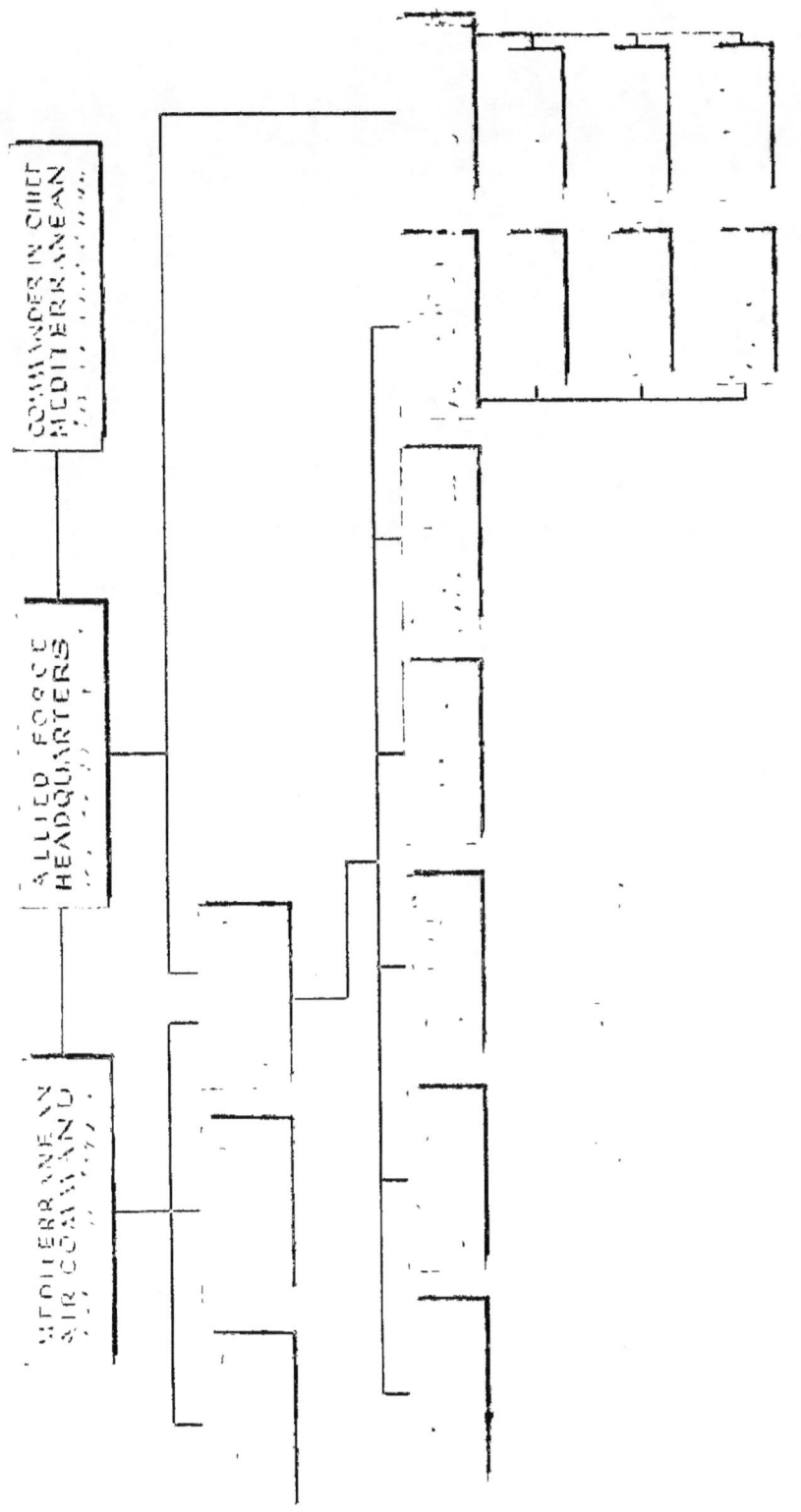

ORGANIZATION OF NORTHWEST AFRICAN AIR FORCES AND ALLIED COMMANDS, 18 FEB 1943

RAF, and was temporarily commanded by Group Capt. G. G. Barrett until the appointment of Air Vice Marshal Hugh P. Lloyd. Air Marshal Lloyd set up headquarters in Algiers where he shared an operations room with Admiral Cunningham.

The Training Command fell to General Cannon, who, since RAF training was mainly carried on in the Middle East, concerned himself for the most part with newly arrived American units. Under his jurisdiction were a large number of airfields in Morocco and western Algeria. XII Air Force Service Command and the maintenance organization of Eastern Air Command were combined as Northwest African Air Service Command under General Dunton. Last of the combined organizations set up on 18 February was Lt. Col. Elliott Roosevelt's Northwest African Photographic Reconnaissance Wing, comprising the U. S. 3d Photographic Group and No. 682 P. R. Squadron, RAF. Colonel Roosevelt's priorities were set by NAAF, in conjunction with AFHQ and MAC, for all work for Washington and London.

General Spaatz drew his staff from the former headquarters of Allied Air Force, Twelfth Air Force, and Eastern Air Command. Air Marshal Robb carried over from Allied Air Force as Deputy and as commander of the RAF element. For the rest, British and American officers were "interleaved." General Spaatz left an administrative echelon at Algiers and set up an operational headquarters at Constantine, where he was in close touch with General Doolittle.[10]

The Significance of NAAF

The advent of Northwest African Air Forces extended, to a great degree, the use of combined British-American headquarters which had been inaugurated by General Eisenhower's AFHQ back in July and August of 1942. Moreover, in NAAF the practice was applied to and below the Command level as British and American personnel intermingled in the common effort. The upshot was a fruitful exchange of ideas and techniques, the submerging of national differences, and the promotion of mutual understanding.

Of equal importance were the functional principles involved in the NAAF organization, especially the provision of separate yet cooperating commands for the tasks of strategic bombardment and air-ground cooperation. This principle was later widely applied in the major theaters of the war, with the result that whole U. S. air forces became strategic air forces—e.g., the Eighth, Fifteenth, and Twentieth—while the Ninth and Twelfth evolved into strictly tactical air forces, concerned with cooperation with the ground forces.

The following lessons had been learned in the indecisive winter of 1942-1943. First, that fighters were necessary for defense of ports and shipping, for bomber escort, for cooperation with the ground forces, and that the standard U. S. fighter command could not oversee all these activities. No more could bombers be segregated under a bomber command, when they were required for such diverse purposes as anti-submarine sorties, strategic bombardment, and strikes on enemy artillery positions. Equally, the elements of the air forces cooperating with the land battle had to be under a single air commander since the planes, unlike the ground components, moved freely over the battleground and could be employed in any part of it. The formation of Allied Air Support Command constituted the formal recognition in Africa of this principle of warfare.[11]

In summation, then, the organizational history of the Twelfth Air Force had passed through three main phases. As set up for TORCH, all fighters, except those under XII ASC, had been under XII Fighter Command; all bombers, except those under XII ASC, had been under XII Bomber Command. This arrangement had simplified training and administration in England when the Twelfth's combat units were under the tutelage of VIII Bomber Command and VIII Fighter Command. General Doolittle's 11 December reorganization into area composite commands had attempted to solve the problems of standing by for trouble with Spanish Morocco--originally the Twelfth's primary commitment--of administering the vast African area, and of reinforcing the Eastern Air Command in the struggle to eject the Axis from Tunisia. NAAF cast the organization into enduring forms by establishing functional rather than area commands, and coalesced the Eastern Air Command and the Twelfth, already yoked under Allied Air Force.[12]

In fact, so coalesced were the two air forces that the Twelfth had apparently evaporated. Its commanding general, Doolittle, expressed the opinion that as soon as certain problems such as outstanding cases before courts martial had been dealt with, the "skeleton" of the Twelfth which would "consist of the name only" would have to be returned to the United States to be reformed, or else be abandoned through War Department orders. In the latter case, if needed in the future, the Twelfth Air Force would have to be reactivated. The basis for his view was that all units, personnel, and equipment of the Twelfth had been given over to the several NAAF formations and its functions had passed to Headquarters, NAAF. As the administrative history of the Twelfth put it: "Both on paper and in actuality it [the Twelfth Air Force] seemed to have disappeared."

However, the Twelfth's headquarters was to live on as the administrative headquarters for the U. S. elements of NAAF, although no staff appointments were made to Headquarters, Twelfth Air Force, as such. Instead it was assumed that the staff appointments to NAAF of 20 February automatically placed those named USAAF officers in the equivalent staff positions of the Twelfth. On 1 March, General Spaatz succeeded General Doolittle in command of the shadow air force.[13]

Something more than a truly allied air force, efficiently organized according to function, was activated on 18 February. With the appearance of NAAF, the air passed to full partnership with the ground and naval forces. Moreover, the appointment of Tedder as head of MAC and of Coningham to command the Tactical Air Force under NAAF brought in the two men who had solved the problems of cooperating with the land battle during the extended struggle with the Afrika Korps.

These points deserve some elaboration.

On 16 February, at Army exercises at Tripoli, Air Marshal Coningham, following General Montgomery as speaker, addressed a group of American and British officers on the general subject of air-ground cooperation. The Eighth Army commander had talked on the same theme, but the air marshal wished to amplify because, as he said, he attached great importance to proper doctrine. He stated the desert-evolved doctrine as follows:

> The Soldier commands the land forces, the Airman commands the air forces; both commands work together and operate their respective forces in accordance with a combined Army-Air plan, the whole operations being directed by the Army Commander.

The air marshal then discussed the fruitful applications of this doctrine during the long punishment of Rommel after El Alamein. However, he went on to say that he had just returned from England and found the "home doctrine" of army-air operations confused. He traced this misfortune to a "mutual petulance" arising from the fact that the inactive home army was constantly calling for aircraft for training purposes which the RAF, in continuous combat, did not feel it could spare. This bad feeling, said Coningham, had been transferred to Africa—its net result, the misuse of the air in the Tunisian operations. In the planning for TORCH, the lessons of the Western Desert had been ignored.[14]

Details of the "misuse" of air power in the early days in Tunisia are furnished in the reports of General Kuter, who, after serving as CG, Allied Air Support Command, went on as Coningham's deputy in the

Tactical Air Force. Kuter did not apologize for the air forces, which had made such egregious mistakes as bombing an RAF field, as well as friendly corps and army headquarters, and had attempted to exculpate themselves by blaming the prevailing system, under which the supporting air was subordinate to the ground commanders. However, Kuter specifically stated that this form of ground force control had delayed victory.

He drew an example from the career of 242 Group, which had been under the "practical command" of the First Army. 242 Group had been successfully operating its Bisleys in night attacks against ports and roads. The Bisley was comparatively slow, armed with .303-cal. machine guns, and entirely unsuitable for daylight operations. However, at one point, the ground commander ordered a squadron out for a daylight attack on an airdrome being utilized by the detested Stukas. The RAF wing commander demurred, but was overruled. He thereupon selected a very able unit--it took off and not a plane returned. Kuter cited another case. An American ground commander drew up plans for dislodging the Axis from Faid Pass. He insisted that a continuous cover of 12 fighters be kept circling over the battle area during all daylight hours, despite the airmen's proof that such action would ground available A-20's requiring escort and preclude reconnaissance or offensive fighter action. Kuter further charged that along the Tunisian front each ground commander had his own assigned air force and had committed the hoary error of restricting its action to the defense of his own area; the outnumbered

Luftwaffe was thus able to muster superior strength at successive vital points.[15]

Such practices came to an end with the appointment of Air Marshal Coningham. As earnest of this development may be taken his cable of 19 February, in which he reported that he had informed First Army and the three corps headquarters that defensive cover flying was being stopped except when authority for it was specifically issued from NATAF. Consistently enough, he soon drew up an operational directive to his subordinate commanders, which passed on to them the Western Desert experience. Melioration of "air support," however, did not occur overnight. It waited on such matters as equipping XII ASC with adequate transportation and radar and improving tactical reconnaissance by turning back the reconnaissance squadrons to their proper work. Both 242 Group's Hurricanes and XII ASC's P-39's, the 154th Observation Squadron, had been employed in ground support work, with a definite deterioration of their reconnaissance value.[16]

Hereafter, then, a new phase of the air war and, consequently, of the ground war began. In the large, the North African winter campaign had merely provided seasoning for all participating American arms;* how valuable the seasoning, was demonstrated by sequels from Sicily to Normandy. The capacity of a military machine to learn from its mistakes, to absorb superior doctrine and technique from whatever

---

* In a staff meeting on 21 December 1942, Doolittle estimated that 75 per cent, "at least," of Twelfth Air Force personnel were either untrained or partially trained.

source derived, is a condition of its continued existence. NAAF and MAC learned so well that they not only survived in full vigor but in time rendered impotent the opposing Luftwaffe. Their successors, but slightly modified from the NAAF-MAC pattern, bore full share in the final passing of Axis power from the Mediterranean basin.

GLOSSARY

AASC	Allied Air Support Command
ADW	Air Defense Wing
AFHQ	Allied Force Headquarters
AFSC	Air Force Service Command
AFCHO	AAF Historical Office
AOC-in-C	Air Officer Commanding-in-Chief
ASC	Air Support Command
CACW	Central Algerian Composite Wing
CCS	Combined Chiefs of Staff
CP	Command Post
CPS (CSP)	Combined Planners Staff (Combined Staff Planners)
EAC	Eastern Air Command
ETO	European Theater of Operations
ETOUSA	European Theater of Operations, U. S. Army
GAF	German Air Force
IAF	Italian Air Force
JCS	Joint Chiefs of Staff
LOC	Line of Communications
LSI	Landing Ship, Infantry
MAC	Mediterranean Air Command
ME	Middle East
MTAF	Mediterranean Tactical Air Force
NAAF	Northwest African Air Forces
NASAF	Northwest African Strategic Air Force
NATAF	Northwest African Tactical Air Force
NATOUSA	North African Theater of Operations, U. S. Army
OPD	Operations Division, War Department General Staff
PR	Photo Reconnaissance
RAF	Royal Air Force
RCT	Regimental Combat Team
SAC	Service Area Command
SASO	Senior Air Staff Officer
Sitrep	Situation Report
STF	SATIN Task Force
UK	United Kingdom (Great Britain)
WACW	Western Algerian Composite Wing

NOTES

Chapter I

1. See AAFRH-5, *Air Phase of the North African Invasion, November 1942*.

Chapter II

1. "Draft of Commander in Chief's Dispatch, North African Campaign" [Eisenhower's Report], in AFSHO files.

2. AAFRH-5, Chap. III.

3. CM-IN-12994 (11-30-42), London to AGWAR, #402, 29 Nov. 1942.

4. AAFRH-5, Chap. III.

5. Ltr., Brig. Gen. J. H. Doolittle to Lt. Gen. H. H. Arnold, 19 Nov. 1942, in AAG 312.1-A, Operations Letters.

6. *Ibid.*; War Diary, 97th Bomb Gp.; histories of 1st, 14th, 31st, and 52d Fighter Gps.

7. Interview with Brig. Gen. G. P. Saville, 5 Jan. 1943; Eisenhower's Report.

8. *Ibid.*; CM-IN-5216 (11-12-42), London to AGWAR, #JAN 359, 12 Nov. 1942.

9. AFHQ to AGWAR, cablegram #4140, 27 Oct. 1942; AFCP to ABFOR, cablegram #248, 10 Nov. 1942. The story of the 60th Troop Carrier Group's D-day mission at Oran can be found in AAFRH-5, Chap. III.

10. Commandeth Gibraltar to AFHQ, cablegram #148GIB, 8 Nov. 1942; First Army to AFCP, cablegram #016, 11 Nov. 1942; supporting documents to history, 64th Troop Carrier Gp.; "History of the 51st Troop Carrier Wing and Components from Activation to 15 May 1943," in "The Twelfth Air Force in the Invasion of Northwest Africa--History of the Twelfth Air Force, Volume I" [Theater History, vol. I].

11. *Ibid.*; CM-IN-5850 (11-14-42), London to AGWAR, cablegram #457, 13 Nov. 1942; Eisenhower's Report.

12. Ibid.; AFHQ to AGWAR, cablegram #643, 15 Nov. 1942.

13. CM-IN-5850 (11-14-42), London to AGWAR, cablegram #457, 13 Nov. 1942; AFCP to CTF, cablegram #223, 10 Nov. 1942; history, 60th Troop Carrier Gp.

14. Ibid.

15. CM-IN-7042 (11-16-42), London to AGWAR, cablegram #JAN 678, 16 Nov. 1942; Supporting documents to history, 64th Troop Carrier Gp.

16. Eisenhower to C's-in-C ME, cablegram #719, 16 Nov. 1942; Eisenhower's Report.

17. Ibid.; AFCP to CG ETF, cablegram #741, 17 Nov. 1942.

18. Hq. 12th AF, Air Intelligence Report [AIR] #19, 29 Nov. 1942; CM-OUT-7113 (11-22-42), TAG to CG ETO, cablegram #R3425, 21 Nov. 1942; ltr., Doolittle to Arnold, 19 Nov. 1942.

19. Ibid.; Air Vice-Marshal Saunders to CP AFHQ, unnumbered cablegram, 17 Nov. 1942.

20. Ltr., Doolittle to Arnold, 19 Nov. 1942; War Diary, 97th Bomb Gp.; History, 14th Fighter Gp.

21. CM-IN-9756 (11-23-42) and CM-IN-11069 (11-26-42), London to AGWAR, cablegrams #JAN 1132 and #571, 22 and 26 Nov. 1942; Eisenhower from Welsh, cablegram unnumbered, 23 Nov. 1942.

22. Ltr., Maj. Gen. Carl Spaatz to Lt. Gen. H. H. Arnold, 23 Nov. 1942, in AAG 312.1-A, Opns. Ltrs.

23. AFCP to EAC, cablegram #921, 19 Nov. 1942; Algiers to AFCP, cablegram unnumbered, 21 Nov. 1942.

24. War Diary, 97th Bomb Gp.

25. Histories, 60th Troop Carrier Gp. and 14th Fighter Gp.; ltr., Maj. Gen. James H. Doolittle to Maj. Gen. George E. Stratemeyer, 31 Jan. 1943, in AAG 312.1-A, Opns. Ltrs.; General Eisenhower's review of North African situation, Anfa Conference, 1st Mtg., 15 Jan. 1943, in J/CCS Div., AFAEP.

26. Ibid.; AAFRH-5, Chap. III; interview with Lt. Norman Segal, 5 Mar. 1943.

27. Histories, 1st Fighter Gp. and 27th Fighter Sq.

28. Algiers to USFOR, London, cablegram #624, 25 Nov. 1942; Eisenhower's Report.

29. Ibid.; CM-IN-11894 (11-28-42), London to AGWAR, cablegram #704, 27 Nov. 1942; David Rame, Road to Tunis, pp. 154-56.

30. History, 52d Fighter Gp.; CM-IN-10054 (11-23-42), Gibraltar to AGWAR, cablegram #1183, 23 Nov. 1942; "Tunisian Encounter," in Hq. RAF, ME, RAF Middle East Review, No. 2 (January-March 1943), p. 24; AIR #29, 9 Dec. 1942.

31. Eisenhower to C's-in-C ME, cablegram #719, 16 Nov. 1942; AIR #16, 24 Nov. 1942.

32. Ibid., #17 and 19, 25 and 29 Nov. 1942; CM-IN-12664 (11-30-42), London to AGWAR, #817, 29 Nov. 1942; interview with Lt. Col. Howard E. Engler, 27 May 1943.

33. Histories, 97th and 301st Bomb Gps., 1st Fighter Gp., and 27th Fighter Sq.; A-3 XII BC to CO XII BC Rear Echelon, Tafaraoui, unnumbered cablegram, 5 Dec. 1942.

34. AIR #16 and #17, 24 and 25 Nov. 1942; interview with Lt. Col. Stephen Avery, 13 Feb. 1943.

35. CM-IN-11545 (11-27-42) and CM-IN-11894 (11-28-42), London to AGWAR, cablegrams #638 and 704, 26 and 27 Nov. 1942; Algiers to USFOR, London, cablegram #624, 25 Nov. 1942.

36. CM-IN-12823 (11-30-42), London to AGWAR, cablegram #822, 29 Nov. 1942.

37. CM-IN-118 (12-1-42), London to AGWAR, cablegram #863, 30 Nov. 1942; Rame, Road to Tunis, p. 177.

38. "History of the 51st Troop Carrier Wing and Components from Activation to 15 May 1943;" Rame, Road to Tunis, p. 176.

39. Ibid., pp. 176-79.

40. CM-IN-118 (12-1-42), London to AGWAR, cablegram #863, 30 Nov. 1942; Hq. 12th AF, Weekly Air Intelligence Summary, #3 and #4, 5 and 12 Dec. 1942; Eisenhower's Report.

41. CM-IN-12664 (11-30-42) and CM-IN-423 (12-2-42), London to AGWAR, cablegrams #817 and 939, 29 Nov. and 1 Dec. 1942; AIR #21 and 22, 1 and 2 Dec. 1942.

42. History, 319th Bomb Gp.

43. Lt. Col. Boyd Hubbard, "Observer's Report: N.W. Africa and U. K. February and March," /Hubbard's Report/, n.d., in Air AG 370.5 (Sec. II--Cases 116 to 192); AIR #19, 29 Nov. 1942.

44. History, 319th Bomb Gp.; AIR #21 and 22, 1 and 2 Dec. 1942.

45. Ibid.; #20-22, 30 Nov.-2 Dec. 1942.

46. First Army CP to AFHQ, unnumbered cablegram, 2 Dec. 1942; Eisenhower's Report.

47. AIR #23, 3 Dec. 1942.

48. Ibid.; cf., history, 310th Bomb Gp.

49. AIR #23, 3 Dec. 1942.

50. CM-IN-2031 (12-5-42), Algiers to AGWAR #1194, 4 Dec. 1942; Eisenhower's Report.

51. AFHQ to AGWAR, cablegram #1110, 3 Dec. 1942; CCS to Eisenhower, Freedom Algiers, cablegram #23, 5 Dec. 1942.

52. AIR #24 and 25, 4 and 5 Dec. 1942.

53. CM-IN-2312 (12-6-42), Algiers to War, cablegram #1224, 5 Dec. 1942; AIR #25 and 29, 5 and 9 Dec. 1942.

54. Ibid., #26, 6 Dec. 1942.

55. AFHQ to USFOR, cablegram #1968, 14 Dec. 1942; First Army CP to AFHQ, cablegram unnumbered, 9 Dec. 1942; Eisenhower's Report.

Chapter III

1. AFHQ to USFOR, cablegram #1968, 14 Dec. 1942; Eisenhower's Report.

2. Ibid.; AAF Historical Studies: No. 30, Ninth Air Force Participation in the Desert Campaign to 23 January 1943, Chap. IV.

3. AFHQ to AGWAR, cablegram #1110, 3 Dec. 1942; Eisenhower's Report; "The Twelfth Air Force in the Tunisian Campaign--History of the Twelfth Air Force, Volume II," [Theater History, vol. II], p. 1-2; Rame, Road to Tunis, p. 153.

4. Ibid., pp. 108-15; history, 14th Fighter Gp.

5. Interview with Brig. Gen. Lawrence S. Kuter, 15 June 1943; see ltr., Brig. Gen. Paul M. Robinett to Gen. George C. Marshall, 8 Dec. 1942, with attached papers, in WP-III-F12, Off. Services Br., AFAEP.

6. Memo, WDOPD to CG AAF, 22 Dec. 1942, sub.: Defense against Dive Bombing, ibid.; AFHQ to AGWAR, cablegram #1110, 3 Dec. 1942; First Army CP to AFHQ, cablegram unnumbered, 3 Dec. 1942.

7. Rame, Road to Tunis, pp. 135-36; AIR 527, 7 Dec. 1942; CP First Army to EAC, cablegram unnumbered, 3 Dec. 1942.

8. Interview with Gen. Saville; interview with Brig. Gen. D. A. Davison, 1 June 1943.

9. CM-IN-2957 (12-6-42), Algiers to War, cablegram #1312, 6 Dec. 1942.

10. AFHQ Operation Memo #27, 20 Oct. 1942, in files of North African Sec., Theater Gp., WDOPD; memo, Maj. Gen. Muir S. Fairchild, DR to CG SOS, 30 Aug. 1942, in Air AG 320.2, Twelfth Air Force; Brig. Gen. S. C. Godfrey to CG AAF, "Report on Airdromes and Aviation Engineers in North Africa," 4 Jan. 1943, in WP-III-F12, Off. Services Br., AFAEP; interview with Gen. Davison.

11. Ibid.; interview with Brig. Gen. S. C. Godfrey, 7 Jan. 1943.

12. "Engineer History, First Army," in Operations Br., AGO, Secret and Confidential Sec., Analysis Files Subsec. [AGO Op. Br. files], 101-43.1.

13. Doolittle to CG XII BC, cablegram #413, 13 Dec. 1942; Doolittle to CO's XII BC and Air Base Telergma, cablegram #468E, 14 Dec. 1942; interview with Gen. Davison.

14. Ibid.; Doolittle to CG XII BC, cablegram #413, 13 Dec. 1942.

15. Interview with Gen. Saville; interview with Gen. Godfrey; Cannon to CG 12th AF, cablegram #0334, 4 Jan. 1943.

16. Ibid.; interview with Gen. Davison; AFHQ to USFOR, cablegram #3727, 1 Jan. 1943; AIR #28, 8 Dec. 1943.

17. Interview with Gen. Godfrey; Eisenhower's Report.

18. AFHQ to USFOR, cablegram #3727, 1 Jan. 1943.

19. ETF to AFHQ, cablegram #0566, 15 Dec. 1942; ETF to AFHQ, cablegram unnumbered, 16 Dec. 1942; AFHQ to Adv. Hq., First Army, cablegram #2133, 16 Dec. 1942; Eisenhower's Report.

20. Ninth Air Force Participation in the Desert Campaign, pp. 84-86; "Malta's Contribution," in RAF Middle East Review, No. 2 (January-March 1943), p. 67; Theater History, vol. II, p. 6.

21. AFHQ to AGWAR, cablegram #1110, 3 Dec.; AFHQ, Air Staff to ABFOR, cablegram #1311, 6 Dec.; ETO, London to AFHQ, cablegram #389, 6 Dec.; London to AFHQ, cablegram #382, 7 Dec.; Middle East to Air Ministry, cablegram #253, 7 Dec.; AFHQ, Air Staff to Air Ministry, cablegram #1448, 8 Dec.; AFHQ, Air Staff to Middle East, cablegram #1450, 8 Dec.; AFHQ, Air Staff to Air Ministry, cablegram #1449, 8 Dec.; EAC CP to First Army CP, cablegram #A74, 5 Dec. 1942; S/Ldr. Eric M. Summers, Blida's Bombers, pp. 8-10, in AFSHO files.

22. Histories, 2d Bomb Div. and 3d Bomb Wing.

23. Ibid.; AIR #34 and 35, 14 and 15 Dec. 1942; Ninth Air Force Participation in the Desert Campaign, pp. 85-86; CM-IN-11370 (1-25-43), Cairo to AGWAR, cablegram #AMSME 4090, 20 Jan. 1943.

24. AFHQ to ABFOR, cablegram unnumbered, about 24 Nov. 1942; ltr., Maj. Gen. Ira C. Eaker to Maj. Gen. Geo. E. Stratemeyer, 6 Dec. 1942, in Air AG 370.2, Bolero; history, XII Bomber Command; Historical Sec., 12th AF, Twelfth Air Force Administrative History, Part I /Administrative History/.

25. Doolittle to CO XII BC, Constantine, message unnumbered, 31 Dec. 1942.

26. Interview with Col. Engler.

27. AIR #33, 34, and 35, 12, 13, and 14 Dec. 1942; CM-IN-10169 (12-24-42), London to War #911, 22 Dec. 1942.

28. Ltr., Maj. Gen. J. H. Doolittle to Lt. Gen. H. H. Arnold, 30 Nov. 1942, in WP-III-F12; interview with Lt. Col. P. W. Tibbetts, 20 Feb. 1943.

29. AIR #36, 16 Dec. 1942.

30. CM-IN-10169 (12-24-42), London to War #911, 22 Dec. 1942; AIR #38 and 39, 18 and 19 Dec. 1942.

31. Ibid., #42, 43, and 44, 22, 23, and 24 Dec. 1942.

32. History, 1st Fighter Gp. The Twelfth Air Force Administrative History, Part III, vol. 1 cites a Twelfth Air Force order of 21 November assigning the 14th Fighter Group to XII Bomber Command. Since the 14th went to Youks on the next day, it assumed that the order was revoked.

33. Interview with Col. Engler; ltr., Doolittle to Arnold, 30 Nov. 1942.

34. Histories, 5th Bomb Wing, 47th Bomb Wing, and 97th Bomb Gp.; interview with Maj. Joseph W. Sabin, 24 June 1943; Doolittle to CG NGW, cablegram #0209, 3 Jan. 1943.

35. History, 97th Bomb Gp.; AIR #47, 27 Dec. 1942.

36. Ibid., #48-52, 28 Dec. 1942-1 Jan. 1943.

37. Histories, 97th Bomb Gp. and 1st and 52d Fighter Gps.; AIR #54, 3 Jan. 1943.

38. Ibid., #57 and 60, 6 and 9 Jan. 1943; Hq. MAAF, A-2 Sec. Special Report 53, "Bomb Damage, Ferryville Naval Base," June 1943, in files AC/AS-2, Air Information Div., Library Br.

39. Capt. William R. Gridley, "B-25s over Italy," AAFSAT in Intel. Rpt., #24, March 1944.

40. Histories, 310th and 319th Bomb Gps.

41. AIR #33, 34, and 38, 13, 14, and 18 Dec. 1942.

42. Ibid., #36 and 39, 16 and 19 Dec. 1942.

43. Middle East to AFHQ, cablegram unnumbered, 14 Dec. 1942.

44. AIR #51 and 52, 31 Dec. 1942 and 1 Jan. 1943.

45. History, 310th Bomb Gp.; AIR #53 and 56, 2 and 5 Jan. 1943.

46. Ibid., #56, 5 Jan. 1943.

47. Ibid., #57-60, 6-9 Jan. 1943.

48. Ibid., 34, 54, and 60, 14 Dec. 1942, 3, 9 Jan. 1943.

49. History, 31st Fighter Gp.; history, Hq. and Hq. Sq. XII Fighter Command; Hq. XII FC, A-2 and A-3 Journals; Theater History, vol. II, p. 9; Doolittle to Col. Blackburn, cablegram #556, 15 Dec. 1942.

50. CM-IN-11394 (11-28-42), London to AGWAR, 704, 27 Nov. 1942; AFHQ to OP ATF, cablegram #1221, 5 Dec. 1942; Doolittle to CG XII BC, cablegram #569, 17 Dec. 1942; AFHQ, Air Staff to AOC EAC, for Lawson, 242 Gp., cablegram #2159, 16 Dec. 1942; EAC Adv. Hq. to AFHQ, cablegram #1, 25 Dec. 1942.

51. Capt. Philip Ayres, "P-38's in the Mediterranean," in AAFSAT Intel. Rpt. #27, May 1944.

52. Doolittle to WACW, cablegram #0266 and Doolittle to CG XII BC, cablegram #0289, 4 Jan. 1943; interviews with Lt. Col. C. C. Kazelman et al, 4 Mar. 1943, Lt. James W. Stubbs, n.d., and Lt. Norman Segal, 5 Mar. 1943.

53. AIR #23, 3 Dec. 1942; histories, 1st and 14th Fighter Gps. and 47th Light Bomb Gp.

54. Ibid.; interview with Capt. Clarence A. Martin, 27 Feb. 1943; Capt. Richard Boonisar, "A-20s Supporting Ground Forces," in AAFSAT Intel. Rpt. #27, May 1944; Blackburn to CG 12th AF, cablegram #0045, n.d.

55. History, 33d Fighter Gp.; A. J. Liebling, "Guerilla from Erie, Pa.," in New Yorker, 13 Feb. 1943, p. 26; interview with Lt. Col. Philip C. Cochran, 3 June 1943.

56. Ibid.; interview with Lt. Col. Vincent Sheean, 3 June 1943.

57. Interview with Lt. Col. Cochran; history, 47th Light Bomb Gp.

58. Ibid.; Air Intelligence Reports for the period.

59. AIR #33 and 35, 13 and 15 Dec. 1942; interview with Col. Cochran.

60. AIR #35, 37, 38 and 40, 15, 17, 18, and 20 Dec. 1942; history, 47th Light Bomb Gp.

61. AIR #39, 40, 42, 49, and 51, 19, 20, 22, 29, and 31 Dec. 1942.

62. Ibid., #52, 54, and 55, 1, 3, and 4 Jan. 1943.

63. Ibid., #55 and 56, 4 and 5 Jan. 1943; CM-IN-1896, Algiers to War, #4200, 4 Jan. 1943; history, 47th Light Bomb Gp.; Doolittle to Baker and Brereton, cablegram #0280 4 Jan. 1943.

64. Ibid.; AIR #58-60, 7-9 Jan. 1943; Doolittle to Baker and Brereton, cablegram #0521, 7 Jan. 1943.

65. AFHQ Operation Memo #30, Organization of North African Theater, 24 Oct. 1942; CM-IN-12994 (11-30-42), London to AGWAR, #402, 29 Nov. 1942.

66. Allied Force Adv. Hq. to CG's CTF, WTF, cablegram #443, 23 Nov. 1942; ltr., Doolittle to Arnold, 19 Nov. 1942.

67. General Eisenhower's review of North African situation, Anfa Conference, 1st Mtg., 15 Jan. 1943.

68. Ltr., Doolittle to Arnold, 19 Nov. 1942.

69. Theater History, vol. II, p. 9-10; "History of I Air Service Area Command (Sp)," p. 34; "Historical Notes on XII Air Support Command . . .," 10 Dec. 1942; Administrative History; Hq. Army Air Forces Service Command, MTO, "History of the Original XII Air Force Service Command . . .," pp. 90-91.

70. Ibid., 91-94; "History of I Air Service Area Command (Sp)," pp. 31-34; Administrative History.

71. Interview with Gen. Saville.

72. Eisenhower's Report; AFHQ to CTF, cablegram #1295, 6 Dec. 1942; AFHQ to USFOR for NTF, cablegram #4703, 8 Jan. 1943.

73. Administrative History; AFHQ, Air Staff to CG WTF, cablegram #738, 28 Nov. 1942. The establishment of the Detachment, XII ASC, traces to AFHQ's directive for BACKBONE II, the combined action of the Fifth Army and the Northern Task Force against Spanish Morocco, for which General Clark would assume command of the NTF. The directive, dated 24 December, specified that the Air Corps detachment for the Fifth Army would consist of a headquarters and sufficient air support communications squadrons to control the three groups initially on call for the operation. On 6 January the Detachment, XII Air Support Command was set up. Commanded by Col. Rosenham Beam, it included initially Detachment Headquarters and Headquarters Squadron, XII ASC, the 2d Air Support Communications Squadron, a provisional air support signal battalion, and the 68th Observation Group. Not long after Colonel Beam arrived at Oujda, BACKBONE was abandoned and insurance against enemy action

via Spain reduced. On 1 March, Detachment, XII ASC was relieved from attachment to the Fifth Army and assigned to the Northwest African Training Command. Hq., Fifth Army, Fifth Army History, Part I . . .; ABFOR to AFCP, Gib., cablegram unnumbered, 16 Nov. 1942; Doolittle to Col. Beam, cablegram #875, 21 Dec. 1942; Doolittle to CO, MCW, cablegram #1033, 12 Jan. 1943; history, XII Air Support Command; Hq. XII ASC, "Report on Operations Conducted by XII Air Support Command, 13 Jan.-9 April 1943" /XII ASC Report/; GO #8, 1 March 1943, Hq. NAAF; AFHQ, Directive for Backbone II, 24 Dec. 1942, in AFSHO files.

74. Theater History, vol. II, pp. 9-10; Administrative History.

75. Memo for Gen. Arnold by Col. Morris R. Nelson, Acting Dir. Air Defense, 20 Nov. 1942, A Plan for Air Defense of Vital Defense Areas, North African Theater, in AAG 381A, War Plans; CM-OUT-9463 and 9464 (11-29-42), WDOPD to USFOR, #R3755 and R3756, 30 Nov. 1942; CM-IN-2012 (12-5-42), Algiers to War #1199, 4 Dec. 1942; CM-IN-2658 (12-6-42), Algiers to War, #1293, 6 Dec. 1942; CM-IN-9272 (12-21-42), Algiers to AGWAR, #2619, 20 Dec. 1942; CM-IN-12940 (28 Jan. 43), Algiers to War #7567, 27 Jan. 1943; histories, 62d, 63d, and 64th Fighter Wings; memo, Maj. Gen. Geo. E. Stratemeyer, C/AS to TAG, 6 Dec. 1942, Air Defense Wings for North Africa, in Air AG 320.2-Africa; ltr., Brig. Gen. G. P. Saville to Maj. Gen. James H. Doolittle, 28 Jan. 1943, in AAG 312.1-A Opns. Ltrs.; Hq. XII FC, A-2 and A-3 Journals; "History of 1 Air Service Area Command (Sp)," p. 35; Theater History, vol. II, 9.

Chapter IV

1. See AAFRH-2, The Origins of the Eighth Air Force: Plans, Organization, Doctrine, Chap. I.

2. CCS 94, 24 July 1942.

3. Memo for Arnold by ACM Sir Charles Portal, 20 Aug. 1942, in Air AG 311.2, Misc. Communication by Wire.

4. Memo for CG ETOUSA by Spaatz, Modification of Basic Policy for the Build-up of U. S. Forces in U. K., 22 Aug. 1942, in Off. Serv. Br., AFAEP; JCS, 32d Meeting, 8 Sep. 1942.

5. Spaatz' Diary, 21 Oct. 1942, in Hq. USSTAF, "Command and Control of U. S. Army Air Forces in Europe."

6. Digest of a conversation between Generals Eisenhower and Spaatz, Widewings, 29 Oct. 1942, sub.: Air Command in the European Air Theater, and Spaatz' Diary, 2 Nov. 1942, in ibid.

7. Ltr., Spaatz to Arnold, 31 Oct. 1942, in AAG 312.1-A, Opns. Ltrs.

8. Ltr., Spaatz to Arnold, 23 Nov. 1942 and inclosures: memo for CG ETOUSA by Spaatz, Organization of the Air Forces in ETOUSA, 14 Nov. 1942, in Parton papers, AFSHO files.

9. Ibid.; ltr., Arnold to Eisenhower, 15 Nov. 1942, in Parton papers; CM-IN-10304 (11-24-42), USAFF to AGWAR #183, 24 Nov. 1942. See also unidentified document on organization of air forces in ETO in "General Eaker's Secret File," AFSHO files.

10. Memo for Staff Planners Section Files, Planning for Operations Subsequent to TORCH, 22 Dec. 1942, in 385, CCS 124--Plans and Opns. in Med., ME, and NE, in J/CCS Div., AFAEP.

11. JCS 153, 18 Nov. 1942.

12. OPS 49/1, 27 Nov. 1942.

13. CPS, 39th Mtg., 30 Nov. 1942.

14. CPS, 40th Mtg., 3 Dec. 1942; CPS 49/3, 8 Dec. 1942; CCS 124/1, 30 Dec. 1942.

15. CPS 49/2, 5 Dec. 1942.

16. Ltr., Eaker to Stratemeyer, 6 Dec. 1942; Administrative History.

17. Algiers to ABFOR, London, cablegram #1107, 3 Dec. 1942, in "General Eaker's Secret File;" ltr., Eaker to Stratemeyer, 2 Jan. 1943, in AAG 370.2, Bolero; S/Ldr. J. N. White, "Evolution of Air Command in the Mediterranean," 13 Nov. 1944, in Parton papers; notes by S/Ldr. White for a study on Air Command in the Mediterranean.

18. CCS, Command of Air Forces in North Africa, Memorandum by the representatives of the British Chiefs of Staff, in 210.331 No. Africa 1-5-43, J/CCS Div., AFAEP; Algiers to USFOR, cablegrams #3626 and 3650, 31 Dec. 1942, in "General Eaker's Secret File."

19. AFHQ to AGWAR and USFOR, cablegram #NAF85, 4 Jan. 1943; Theater History, vol. II, p. 10; Administrative history; AFHQ, Directive to Maj. Gen. Carl Spaatz, CG Allied Air Force, 5 Jan. 1943, in Parton papers.

20. R&R, Arnold to Stratemeyer, 17 Dec. 1942, and comment by AFAEP, 1 Jan. 1943, in AAG 312.1-A, Opns. Ltrs.

21. Commander in Chief's Draft Dispatch, Sicilian Operation, in ACO Op. Br. files.

22. CCS 170/2, 23 Jan. 1943, Final Report to the President and Prime Minister Summarizing Decisions by the CCS /Casablanca Conference/.

23. Ibid.; S/Ldr. White, "Evolution of Air Command in the Mediterranean"; CCS 163, 20 Jan. 1943, System of Air Command in the Mediterranean (Proposals of the British Chiefs of Staff).

24. Target: Germany; Lt. Gen. Ira C. Eaker, "Final Report on Eighth Air Force," 11 Jan. 1944, in AFSHO files; CCS, "The Bomber Offensive from the United Kingdom," CCS 166/1/D, 21 Jan. 1943, and "The Case for Day Bombing" etc., in above report.

25. Ltr., Eaker to Stratemeyer, 20 Jan. 1943, in AAG 312.1-B, Opns. Ltrs.; Administrative History.

Chapter V

1. "Ninth Air Force Participation in the Desert Campaign. . . ."

2. Eisenhower's Report; Hq. II Corps, "Report of Operations, II Corps, 1 Jan.-15 Mar. 1943" /II Corps' Report/, 2 May 1943, in AGO Op. Br. files, 202-33.4.

3. Ibid.; AFHQ to II Corps, cablegram #4669, 8 Jan. 1943; General Eisenhower's review of North African situation, Anfa Conference, 1st Mtg., 15 Jan. 1943.

4. Ibid.; AFHQ to II Corps, cablegram #4669, 8 Jan. 1943; Eisenhower's Report.

5. Ibid.; II Corps' Report; Doolittle to CG, XII ASC, cablegram #1335, 17 Jan. 1943; AFHQ G-3 to 12th AF, cablegram #2309, 19 Jan. 1943.

6. Craig to CG 12th AF, cablegrams #816 and 1159, 9 and 11 Jan. 1943; Doolittle to CG, XII ASC, cablegram #0753, 10 Jan. 1943, and cablegram unnumbered, 12 Jan. 1943; History of the Original XII Air Force Service Command.

7. Histories, 52d and 81st Fighter Gps.; Doolittle to CG XII ASC, cablegrams #1275 and 1335, 16 and 17 Jan. 1943; AIR #62, 11 Jan. 1943.

8. AFHQ to C-in-C's MA, cablegram #5986, 17 Jan. 1943; Eisenhower's Report.

9. "Lessons of the Tunisian Campaign 1942-3, British Forces," in AGO Op. Br. files, 99/19-33.4.

10. II Corps' Report; Eisenhower's Report.

11. Ibid.; CM-IN-9169 (20 Jan.), CM-IN-9507 (21 Jan.), CM-IN-11776 (26 Jan.), CM-IN-10874 (24 Jan.), and CM-IN-11318 (25 Jan. 1943), Algiers to War, cablegrams #6321 and unnumbered, 20 Jan.; #6604 and 6739, 22 Jan.; and #6892, 24 Jan. 1943.

12. Eisenhower's Report; AIR #70, 72, and 73, 19, 21, and 22 Jan. 1943; Brig. Gen. L. S. Kuter to CG AAF, "Organization of American Air Forces" /Kuter's Report/, 12 May 1943. The above report is authority for II Corps' refusal to aid XIX Corps. Although General Kuter does not specify the Robaa-Cusseltia action, it is clear from internal evidence that he had this action in reference.

13. II Corps' Report; Freedom, Algiers to Air Ministry, Whitehall, cablegram ACSA #108, 22 Jan. 1943; Eisenhower's Report; XII ASC Report.

14. AFHQ, Air Staff to CG 8th AF, cablegram #1298, 29 Dec. 1942; Baker to Spaatz, cablegram #1357, 30 Dec. 1942; Hq. Allied Air Force to AASC, cablegram unnumbered, 23 Jan. and cablegrams #405 and 3202, 25 and 26 Jan. 1943; Hq. Allied Air Force to CON, cablegram #406, 25 Jan. 1943; Administrative History.

15. Eisenhower's Report; AIR #74 and 75, 23 and 24 Jan. 1943; XII ASC Report.

16. Ibid.

17. Interview with Lt. Col. Sheean; CM-IN-3097 (1-7-43), Algiers to AGWAR, cablegram #4509, 7 Jan. 1943; CM-OUT-4059 (1-12-43), OPD to Freedom Algiers, cablegram #1005, 12 Jan. 1943.

18. AAFRH-5, pp. 38-39; Historical Sec., USSAFE, "Operation Torch: The Dispatch of Aircraft from the United Kingdom of the Eighth Air Force," 14 Sep. 1944; AFHQ to CG 8th AF, cablegram unnumbered, 1 Jan. 1943; CM-OUT-6053 (1-18-43), Hq. AAF to CG AAF, Casablanca, cablegram #123, 18 Jan. 1943; AASC Adv. CP to Allied Air Force, cablegram #14, 4 Feb. 1943; histories, 81st and 350th Fighter Gps.

19. Ibid.; XII ASC Report; Doolittle to CG NOW, cablegram #0631, 8 Jan. 1943; AASC, 18 Army Gp. to Allied Air Force, cablegram #A-521, 15 Feb. 1943.

20. AIR #79-91, 28-30 Jan. 1943; Eisenhower's Report.

21. Ibid.; II Corps' Report; AIR #82, 31 Jan. 43.

22. Rame, Road to Tunis, 228-29; Eisenhower's Report; XII ASC Report; AIR #83 and 84, 1 and 2 Feb. 1943; Kuter's Report.

23. AIR #85, 3 Feb. 1943; Doolittle to CO NOW, cablegram #1567, 20 Jan. 43; Doolittle to CG's XII ASC and XII BC, cablegram #0319, 5 Feb. 1943; Doolittle to CG 1st ADW, cablegram #0420, 7 Feb. 43; XII ASC Report; FAIRFIELD to Allied Air Force, cablegram unnumbered, 1 Feb. 1943; Extracts from inspection trip by Col. John H. McCormick in Northwest Africa, in AAG 370.2, Africa.

24. Eisenhower's Report; II Corps' Report; AIR #86 and 87, 4 and 5 Feb. 43.

25. Edgar McInnis, The War: Fourth Year, pp. 146-47; Spaatz to Doolittle and Kuter, cablegram #8456, 1 Feb. 1943; AASC, Beaver to 12th AF, cablegram #A76, 3 Feb. 1943; AASC, Adv. CP to XII ASC, 242 Gp., Hq. Allied Air Force, and XII BC, cablegram #15, 3 Feb. 1943; AIR #76, 25 Jan. 1943.

26. AIR #83, 85, 86, and 87, 1, 3, 4, and 5 Feb. 1943.

27. AIR #91 and 92, 9 and 10 Feb. 1943.

28. II Corps' Report; AIR #91, 92, 94, and 95, 9, 10, 12, and 13 Feb. 1943.

29. AASC, Beaver to Allied Air Force, cablegram #A136, 7 Feb. 1943; AASC, Beaver to AFHQ, cablegram #A147, 8 Feb. 1943.

30. Freedom, Algiers to AASC, cablegram #204, 11 Feb. 1943; Hq. Allied Air Force to CG AASC, cablegram #0818, 13 Feb. 1943; Adv. CP AASC to AFHQ, cablegram unnumbered, 6 Feb. 1943; Adv. CP AASC to XII ASC, 242 Gp. Hq. Allied Air Force, and XII BC, cablegram #K5, 3 Feb. 1943; AASC to Allied Air Force, cablegrams #A146 and K20, 8 Feb. 1943, and #A519, 12 Feb. 1943; AASC to AFHQ, cablegram #A518, 12 Feb. 1943; ltr., Spaatz to Arnold, 8 Feb. 1943, in AAG 312.1-B, Opns. Ltrs.; Hq. Allied Air Force to CG 8th AF, cablegram #0091, 2 Feb. 1943; Hq. RAF, ME to Freedom, Algiers, cablegram #A0262, 28 Jan. 1943.

Chapter VI

1. Commander in Chief's Draft Dispatch, Sicilian Operation; CCS 151/1, 29 Jan. 1943, Axis Strategy in North Africa; AFHQ to AGWAR, cablegram #4430, 6 Jan. 1943; Eisenhower's Report; Office of NCXF, Algiers, "Review of Situation Regarding Enemy Supplies to Tunisia," 10 Feb. 1943, in AFSHO files; "Malta's Contribution."

2. Ibid.; Eisenhower's Report.

3. Air Intelligence Reports, December 1942-January 1943; AAF Historical Studies: No. 13, The Development of Tactics in the AAF, pp. 36-37; "Masthead Attacks Against Shipping," in AFGIB, July 1943, p. 20; interview with Lt. Col. Engler; Doolittle to CG XII BC, cablegram #0476, 6 Jan. 1943; Cannon to CG 12th AF, cablegram #793, 9 Jan. 1943; ltr., Lt. Gen. Spaatz to Maj. Gen. Stratemeyer, 26 Mar. 1943, in AAG 370.2, Africa; Minutes of Staff Meeting, Hq. 12th AF, 11 Jan. 1943, in AFSHO files.

4. Ibid.; Doolittle to CG/SC, cablegram #0714, 9 Jan. 1943; Air Intelligence Reports; interview with Lt. Col. Engler; "Review of Situation Regarding Enemy Supplies to Tunisia"; "Masthead Attacks Against Shipping," p. 23; Spaatz to Arnold, cablegram #7859, 30 Jan. 1943.

5. AIR #72-75, 21-24 Jan. 1943.

6. Ibid.; 79, 81, 83, and 85, 28 and 30 Jan., 1 and 3 Feb. 1943.

7. "Review of Situation Regarding Enemy Supplies to Tunisia"; O.N.I. Weekly, 29 Mar. 1944, pp. 977-78; AIR #93 and 96, 11 and 14 Feb. 1943.

8. History, 310th Bomb Gp.; AIR #96 and 104-106, 14 and 22-24 Feb. 1943.

9. Interview with Lt. Col. Engler; CCS 159/1, 20 Jan. 1943, "The Bomber Offensive from North Africa."

10. AIR #64 and 67, 13 and 16 Jan. 1943; AC/AC, Intelligence, Impact, May 1943, pp. 26-27.

11. Ibid.; April, pp. 4-5; Hq. PAF, ME to AFHQ, cablegram #A406, 17 Jan. 1943; AIR #61, 64, and 70, 10, 13, and 19 Jan. 1943; ltr., Spaatz to Arnold, 8 Feb. 1943.

12. AIR #74 and 90, 23 Jan. and 3 Feb. 1943; Impact, April 1943, p. 6.

13. Doolittle to CG XII BC, cablegram #1495, 19 Jan. 1943; AIR #66, 71, and 72, 19, 20, and 21 Jan. 1943.

14. Histories, 97th and 301st Heavy Bomb Gps. and 1st and 14th Fighter Gps.

15. AIR #73-76, 22-25 Jan. 1943; Doolittle to CG XII BC, cablegram #0612, 8 Jan. 1943.

16. AIR #80-84, 29 Jan.-2 Feb. 1943.

17. Cannon to CG 12th AF, cablegram #3928, 31 Jan. 1943; Doolittle to CG XII BC, cablegram #0086, 3 Feb. 1943; ltr., Spaatz to Arnold, 8 Feb. 1943; AIR #90, 8 Feb. 1943.

18. AIR #91, 98, and 100-102, 9, 15, and 18-20 Feb. 1943.

19. Hq. 12th AF, "Operations and Statistics of Twelfth Air Force," in AGO Op. Br. files, 107-66.2; AAFRH-5, p. 22; Doolittle to CG AAF, cablegram #64, 6 Dec. 1942; ltr., Doolittle to Arnold, 30 Nov. 1942; ltr., Doolittle to Stratemeyer, 31 Jan. 1943.

20. CM-IN-10053 (12-23-42), Algiers to AGWAR, #2784, 22 Dec. 1942; AAR to AFHQ, cablegram #R3972, 5 Dec. 1942; Doolittle to AGWAR #306, 7 Dec. 1942; ltr., Baker to Stratemeyer, 2 Jan. 1943.

21. Ltr., Arnold to Doolittle, 21 Dec. 1942, in AAG 312.1-A, Opns. Ltrs.; AGWAR to USFOR, London, cablegram #R2371, 22 Oct. 1942; AFHQ to AGWAR, cablegram #4135, 26 Oct. 1942; CM-OUT-4332 (11-13-42), CG AAF to CG ETO, #R3123, 13 Nov. 1942; ATC, Accra to CG 12th AF, cablegram #1148, 27 Dec. 1942.

22. CM-OUT-9078 (12-27-42), OPD to Freedom, Algiers, #513, 26 Dec. 1942; memo, Lt. Col. Emery A. Boudreau, Asst. Chief, Traffic Div., AC/AS, MM&D to AFAEP, Expediting Aircraft to the 12th Air Force, 21 Apr. 1943, in AFSHO files.

23. Cannon to CG 12th AF, cablegrams #1926, 2784, and 2873, 17, 23, and 24 Jan. 1943; Allied Air Force to AGWAR, cablegram #7038, 24 Jan. 1943; Spaatz to CG AASC, cablegram #1299, 19 Feb. 1943; Allied Air Force to USFOR, cablegram #7012, 24 Jan. 1943; Allied Air Forces to AGWAR, cablegram #703, 25 Jan. 1943.

24. Ltrs., Spaatz to Stratemeyer, 2 Feb. 1943, in AAG 312.1-A, Opns. Ltrs., and 26 Mar. 1943, in AAG 370.2, Africa; Hq. NAAF to AGWAR, cablegram #1333, 20 Feb. 1943.

25. Extracts from inspection trip by Col. McCormick; Allied Air Force to AGWAR, cablegram #7158, 25 Jan. 1943; Spaatz to CG 2 ADW, cablegram #1335, 20 Feb. 1943.

26. Hq., NAAF, A-3 Sec., Operations Bulletin #2, p. 8, in AFSHO files; NAAF to Washington, cablegram #1566, 23 Feb. 1943; ltr., Spaatz to Arnold, 17 Feb. 1943, in Off. Serv. Br., AFAEP, WP-III-F12; interview with Lt. Col. Avery.

27. XII ASC Report; interview with Lt. Col. Cochran; AFHQ to TROOPERS, cablegram #6503, 12 Jan. 1943; AFHQ to AGWAR, cablegram #8334, 4 Feb. 1943.

28. Ltr., Spaatz to Stratemeyer, 26 Mar. 1943; Hubbard's Report; comment #4 on ltrs., Spaatz to Arnold, 17 and 19 Feb. 1943, in AAG 312.1-B, Opns. Ltrs.; ltr., Spaatz to Arnold, 17 Feb. 1943.

29. AIR #62, 64, and 66, 11, 13, and 15 Jan. 1943.

30. *Ibid.*, #69, 81, 82, and 96, 18, 30, 31 Jan. and 14 Feb. 1943.

31. History, 12th Bomb Gp.

Chapter VII

1. "Tunisian Encounter"; II Corps' Report; AIR #97, 99, 15, 17 Feb. 1943; AASC, First Army Hq. to XII BC, cablegram #A177, 13 Feb. 43, #A184, 14 Feb. 43; AASC to 12th AF, #A190, 14 Feb. 43; history, 81st Fighter Gp.; Eisenhower's Report.

2. "History of the Original XII Air Force Service Command"; XII ASC Report; Hq. Allied Air Force to CG AASC, cablegram #598, 10 Feb. 43; AASC, First Army Hq. to Allied Air Force, #A200, 14 Feb. 43; AASC, 18 Army Gp. to 12th AF, cablegram #A122, 18 Feb. 43; ltr., Spaatz to Arnold, 19 Feb. 1943.

3. Ibid.; Histories, 31st, 350th, and 81st Fighter Gps. and 47th Bomb Gp.; AIR #100, 18 Feb. 1943.

4. Eisenhower's Report; II Corps' Report; GO #1, Hq. NAAF, 18 Feb. 1943; AASC, 18 Army Gp. to 12th AF, cablegram #A122, 18 Feb. 43; Air Hq. 18 Army Gp. to XII BC, cablegram #A26, 19 Feb. 43.

5. AIR #101, 102, 19, 20 Feb. 1943; Spaatz to CG NATAF, cablegrams #1334 and 1631, 20 and 24 Feb. 1943; Eisenhower's Report; II Corps' Report.

6. Ibid.; Eisenhower's Report; AIR #104 and 105, 22 and 23 Feb. 1943; histories, 47th, 31st, and 81st Fighter Gps.; Hq. XII ASC, Daily Intelligence Summary of Missions, 22 Feb. 1943, in AFSHO files; AASC, First Army Hq. to 242 Gp., cablegram #A298, 21 Feb. 43.

7. "Tunisian Encounter"; Hq. XII ASC, A-2 Periodic, 22 Feb. 1943, in AFSHO files; AIR #106, 24 Feb. 1943; Eisenhower's Report.

8. Ibid.

9. "Evolution of Air Command in the Mediterranean"; Administrative History; AFHQ GO #20, 17 Feb. 1943.

10. Ibid.; MAC GO #1, 18 Feb. 1943; NAAF GO #1, 18 Feb. 1943; NAAF to Commands, cablegram #1655, 24 Feb. 1943; Administrative History; "Evolution of Air Command in the Mediterranean."

11. Ltr., Spaatz to Arnold, 7 Mar. 1943, in AAG 370.2, Africa; "Organization for African Victory," in AFGIB, July 1943.

12. Administrative History.

13. Ibid., pp. 48-50.

14. "Talk of Air Vice-Marshal Sir A. Coningham to Assembled British and American General and Senior Officers at the end of the second day of the Army Exercise," Tripoli, 16 Feb. 1943, Parton papers.

15. Interview with Gen. Kuter; Kuter Report.

16. Air Hq. 18 Army Gp. to XII BC, cablegram #A26, 19 Feb. 1943; MTAF, Report on Operations during the Campaign in Tunisia, in AFSHO files; Air Marshal Coningham, General Operational Directive to OC, XII ASC, AOC No. 242 Gp., AOC AHQ Western Desert, 20 Feb. 1943, in MTAF report.

BIBLIOGRAPHICAL NOTE

Because of the distressing lack of summary material on the early campaigns in Africa, in the preparation of this study extensive recourse was had to message files. These files are of two general types: War Department messages in either AAF Message Center or AFSHO (Historical Office) files, and the messages of the Twelfth Air Force in AFSHO files. War Department messages may be identified by the CM-IN (or CM-OUT) citation. The theater message files are the more valuable and of them the following volumes were consulted: 1-10, 12-16, 24-29, 32, 35, 40-61.

Of the summary material available, constant use was made of General Eisenhower's report on the North African campaign ("Draft of Commander in Chief's Dispatch, North African Campaign") and of II Corps' report on its Tunisian operations ("Report of Operations, II Corps, 1 Jan.-15 Mar. 1943"). Brig. Gen. Lawrence S. Kuter's report to General Arnold on "Organization of American Air Forces," 12 May 1943, is an excellent critique of the early career of air-ground cooperation.

The efforts of the Twelfth Air Force Historical Section are going far to fill the gaps in the story of the first months in Africa. Particularly valuable is the "Twelfth Air Force Administrative History." The activities of XII Air Force Service Command, on which this narrative but lightly touches, are detailed in two studies made by Headquarters Army Air Forces Service Command, Mediterranean Theater of Operations: "History of the Original XII Air Force Service Command . . ." and "History of I Air Service Area Command (Sp)." "History of III Air Service Area Command (Sp)," prepared by Twelfth Air Force, is companion to the above items.

All interviews cited in the notes may be found in Library Branch, Air Information Division, Assistant Chief of Air Staff-2. Also in these files are the Twelfth Air Force Daily Air Intelligence Reports upon which the accounts of air action in this study are based.

INDEX

A

A-20, 70, 72, 74-75, 77-79, 113, 119, 122-26, 130, 164, 168-69, 174-75, 186
A-20B, 72
AC/AS Plans, 104
Accra, 66, 120, 154
Aegean Sea, 94
AFHQ, 12, 98-99, 115, 131, 145, 159, 177-78, 181-82
Afrika Korps, 42-43, 94, 109-10, 148, 163, 184
Agee, Lt. Col. S. W., 64
Ain Beida, 51, 173
Ain M'lila, 147
Airacobra. See P-39.
Air C-in-C, Mediterranean, 106
Air Intelligence Report, 67
Air Support Control, 174
Alaska-Siberia route, 121
Albacore, 135
Aleutians, 136
Alexander, Gen. Sir Harold, 7, 105, 114, 177, 180
Algeria, 8-9, 37, 47, 54, 80, 98, 110, 181
Algiers, 2-4, 7-8, 10-14, 17-20, 22, 25, 29, 46-47, 56, 86, 97-98, 109-10, 132, 134, 151, 178, 181
Allied Air Force, 103, 131, 181
Allied Air Support Comd., 114, 119, 127, 131-32, 166, 183, 185
Allied Force, 109
  Acting Deputy Commander in Chief for Air, 97
Allied Force Headquarters. See AFHQ.
Anderson, Brig. Gen. O. A., 95, 98
Anderson, Gen. K.A.N., 10, 23, 33-34, 40, 44, 51-52, 118, 123, 180
Andrews, Lt. Gen. F. M., 108
Anfa, 104, 107, 116
AOC-in-C, Middle East, 106
AOC-in-C, Northwest Africa, 106
Arabs, 49
Archer, H.M.S., 9, 73, 153

Argonaut, H.M.S., 135
Argus, H.M.S., 11
Ariana, 34
Arnold, Gen. H. H., 80, 88-89, 132, 155
Arzeu, 8-9
Atcham, 121
Atkinson, Brig. Gen. J. H., 24, 60
Atlas mountains, 49
Auchinleck, Gen., 43
Aurora, H.M.S., 135

B

B-17, 10, 18-22, 24-26, 30-31, 33, 37, 39, 49, 55-63, 128-30, 132, 136, 144, 146-48, 150-52, 154, 156, 175-76
B-24, 54-55
B-25, 9, 35, 39-40, 64, 66, 68, 71, 127, 129, 136, 138, 141, 142-43, 146, 149-50, 152, 154, 159-61, 165, 172, 175
B-26, 31-32, 34, 39, 55, 64-68, 127-29, 136, 138-41, 144-46, 149, 151-52, 154, 159-62, 165, 176
BACKBONE, 4
BACKBONE II, 197 (n 73)
Balearics, 134
Balkan area, 94
Barker, Col. J. DeF., 118-19
Barre, Gen., 15-16, 115
Barrett, GC G. G., 181
Bartron, Col. H. A., 83
Bathurst, 66, 154
Bay of Biscay, 107
Beam, Col. Rosenham, 82, 197 (n 73)
Beaufighter, 19, 151
Beja, 40
Ben Gardane, 148
Ben Zina, 68

Berteaux, 66, 71, 147
Beverly, Col. G. H., 83
Biskra, 49, 58-60, 62, 71, 82, 147, 156, 162
Bisley a/c (Blenheim V), 24, 33, 53, 177, 186
Bizerte, 10, 15, 18, 20, 23, 25, 27, 29, 30, 33-34, 37, 41, 52-54, 56-64, 70, 110, 140-41, 148, 150, 163
Blackburn, Brig. Gen. T. W., 69
Black Sea, 94
Blade Force, 13, 33
Blida, 19, 26, 46, 48, 53
Bofors AA, 71, 74
BOLERO, 2
"Bomb Alley," 3, 11, 134
Bone, 3, 11-13, 15, 24, 29-30, 37, 39, 46, 48, 62, 81, 109, 116, 134, 139, 150, 158
Bordj Toual, 129
Boston, 33, 79, 114, 123, 174. See also DB-7.
Bou Arada, 116-17
Bou Chebka, 123
Bou Dries, 173
Bougie, 11, 15, 29, 82
Bou Thadi, 124
British Chiefs of Staff, 2, 100, 102, 133
Broadhurst, Air Vice Marshal Harry, 180
Brooke, Sir Alan, 133
Buerat, 43, 109

C

C-47, 9, 10, 12-15, 21, 28, 49-50, 62
Cagliari, 24, 151
Cagliari-Elmas, 151
Cairo, 132, 178
Camp Mangin, 147
Cani Is., 58, 135
Cannon, Brig. Gen. J. K., 6, 9, 50, 56, 82, 85, 120, 137, 151, 181
Canrobert, 46, 51, 53, 72, 167, 173

Cant Z-506, 143, 153
Cant Z-1007, 138-39
Cap Bon, 115, 136, 142
Cape Zebib, 58
Cap Tenes, 82
Carthage, 65
Casablanca, 4, 6-10, 37, 44, 47, 81, 86-87, 98, 104-05, 118, 126, 131, 133-34, 143, 154, 172, 177
Casablanca Service Area Command (Prov), 83
Castel Benito, 145-46
Cazes, 9
Center Task Force, 4-5, 8, 46-47, 80, 109
Central Algerian Composite Wing, 82-83, 86
Centa, 4
Chateaudun du Rhumel, 60, 147
Chebba, 160
Chenango, U.S.S., 8, 73
Cherichera, 79
Chott Djerid, 113
Chotts, 115
Churchill, Prime Minister Winston, 92-94, 104, 107
C-in-C, Levant, 105
C-in-C, Mediterranean, 105
Clark, Maj. Gen. Mark, 11, 16, 20, 111
Cochran, Maj. Philip, 73, 113
Colonna, Col. J. O., 47
Combat Comd., A, 123-24, 166
Combat Comd. B, 33, 40, 51, 117, 119, 123, 126, 172
Combat Comd. C, 123
Combat Comd. D, 124, 126, 130
Combined Chiefs of Staff, 2, 20, 37, 51, 90, 96, 105-06, 143
Combined Intelligence Committee, 133
Combined Staff Planners, 93, 95-96, 105
Coningham, Air Marshal Sir Arthur, 106, 132, 170-71, 180, 184-85, 187
Constantine, 14, 36, 49, 56, 60, 66, 82, 109, 113, 115-16, 119, 131, 173, 180-81

Constantine Div., 111
Constantine plateau, 147
Constantine Service Area Comd. (Prov), 83
Craig, Brig. Gen. Howard, 20, 85, 111-13, 118, 178-79
Cross, Air Commodore K.B.B., 180
Crosthwaite, Col. J. C., 60
Cunningham, Fleet Adm. Sir Andrew, 43, 98, 105, 134, 141, 177, 181
Cyclope, 63
Cyrenaica, 55

D

Dakar, 7
Darlan, Adm., 13
Davison, Brig. Gen. D. A., 47
Dawson, Air Vice Marshal C. G., 178
DB-7, 22, 24, 32, 34, 38, 40, 46, 56, 70-71, 75-78, 81, 120. See also Boston.
Dean, Lt. Col. F. M., 174
Dechret bou Dabouss, 112, 117
Decimomannu, 152-53
Depienne, 27
Dernaia, 169
Desert Luftwaffe, 127
Deuxieme Bureau, 73
Dewoitine a/c, 12
Djebel Abiod, 16, 40, 150
Djebel bou Dabouss, 130
Djebel Chirich, 117
Djebel Dernaia, 169
Djebel Djelloud marshalling yards, 147
Djebel Hamra, 171
Djebel Krechem, 42
Djebel Ksaira, 165
Djebel Lessouda, 164-65
Djedeida, 23, 27, 29, 32, 35, 43, 133
Djidjelli, 11, 14, 46, 48
Doolittle, Maj. Gen. J. H., 4, 17, 20, 49, 56-57, 59, 80-81, 84, 98-99, 103, 137, 153, 180-81, 183-84, 187
Dorsals, 177. See also Eastern; Western.
Douglas, Air Chief Marshal Sir Sholto, 106, 179

Duncan, Col. C. E., 55
Dunn, Col. A. A., 83
Dunton, Brig. Gen. D. H., 83, 181
Duzerville, 12-13

E

8th Air Force, 6, 54, 71, 88, 90, 92, 100, 103-04, 108, 143, 182
VIII Air Force Service Comd., 121
8th Army, 106, 109-10, 116, 127, 145, 176-77, 185
VIII Bomber Comd., 18, 22, 90, 107, 183
VIII Fighter Comd., 183
11th Brigade, 33, 36
18th Army Gp., 131, 170, 177, 180
81st Bomb Sq., 162
81st Fighter Gp., 113, 119-21, 165, 168, 173, 175
82d Bomb Sq., 162
82d Fighter Gp., 67, 129, 146-47, 151, 161
809th Engineer Bn. (Avn), 47
814th Engineer Bn. (Avn), 47
815th Engineer Bn. (Avn), 47
817th Engineer Bn. (Avn), 47
871st Airborne Engineer Bn. (Avn), 47
888th Airborne Engineer Company (Avn), 112
Eaker, Maj. Gen. I. C., 54, 90, 97, 107, 154
Eastern Air Comd. (EAC), 4-5, 10, 17, 23, 29, 36, 92, 100, 103, 106, 119, 137, 158, 177-79, 181
Eastern Assault Force, 4
Eastern Dorsal, 115, 133, 163
Eastern Task Force, 46
Eglin Field, 136
Egypt, 7
Eisenhower, Gen. D. D., 3, 12, 16, 19-20, 30, 36-37, 40-45, 51-52, 55, 90-94, 97, 99, 102, 105-06, 110-11, 114-15, 133, 136, 155, 158, 177, 182
El Acheila, 42, 109
El Alamein, 7, 185
El Aouina, 19-20, 29-30, 32-34, 38, 55-56, 65, 146, 161

El Aouinet, 78, 161
El Bathan, 39
El Djem, 68
El Guettar, 78, 128
El-Ma-El-biod, 167
Elmas, 24-25, 152
England, 6-7, 19, 22, 26, 31, 35, 47, 70, 94. See also United Kingdom.
English Channel, 96
ETOUSA, 91-92, 105, 108, 154
Evacuation Plan A, 166-67

F

1st Air Defense Wing, 86-87, 180
1st Armored Div., 110-11, 164-65
1st Armored Regt., 165
1st Army, 4, 8, 10, 12, 16, 52, 69, 98-99, 103, 106, 109-11, 115, 170, 177, 180, 186-87
1st Bomb Wing, 118
1st Fighter Gp., 9, 24-25, 37, 58-59, 65, 128-29, 136, 140, 146-49, 151-52
1st Service Area Command, 83
4th Fighter Sq., 113
5th Army, 17, 84-85, 98,
5th Bomb Wing (H), 6, 60
5th FA Bn., 111
5th Leicesters, 172
14th Airfield Construction Gp., 48
14th Fighter Gp., 9, 19, 21-22, 25-26, 44, 69, 71, 112, 138, 142, 146-47, 157, 195a (n 32)
15th Air Force, 143, 182
15th Light Bomb Sq., 10, 22, 32, 70, 157
46th Service Sq., 167-68
47th Bomb Wing (M), 60
47th Light Bomb Gp., 70-72, 74, 78, 112, 120, 125, 162, 173
51st Troop Carrier Wing, 10, 17, 82-84
52d Fighter Gp., 24, 62, 113, 126, 130, 151-53
443d CA Bn., 111
513th Bomb Sq., 55
Faid, 115, 123-26, 130, 132, 176

Faid Pass, 123-24, 126, 133, 163-64, 186
Fedala, 9
Feriana, 66, 73, 123, 164, 169, 171
Feriana-Kasserine road, 175
Ferryville, 56, 63, 150
Fez, 48
Flying Fortress. See B-17.
Focke-Wulf. See FW-190.
Fondouk, 73, 79, 115-16, 126, 130
Force H, 134
Force Q, 134-36, 141
Fort Lamy, 144
Foum Tatahouine, 42
France, 31
Fredendall, Maj. Gen. L. R., 20, 111-12
Free French, 144
French, 13, 15-16, 23, 115-16, 120
French Morocco, 8, 17, 46-47, 60, 72, 80, 98, 126, 181
FW-190, 25, 29-30, 33, 39, 56-58, 60, 63, 70, 75, 125, 128-30, 140, 142, 144-45, 149-50, 152, 157-58, 161, 164

G

Gabes, 16, 26, 29, 32, 35, 38, 42, 59, 66, 69, 75, 77-79, 112, 114-16, 128-30, 144, 147, 160
Gabes-Medenine-Ben Gardane road, 148
Gabes West, 176
Gadames, 144
Gafsa, 75, 112, 115-16, 123, 126, 130, 164, 166-69, 172
Gafsa airfield, 16, 50-51, 69
Gambut, 162
Gambut Main, 55
Gascogne, 63
German Air Force (GAF), 11, 19, 29, 32, 42, 48, 70, 78, 129, 134-35, 153, 158, 161, 175, 178, 187-88
Gibraltar, 3, 7, 10, 12, 18, 20, 92, 134. See also Strait of Gibraltar.

Giraud, Gen., 13, 16, 115
Graiba, 68, 160
Graves, Col. D. D., 87
Greenland, 31
Guelma, 116
Guercif, 48
Gulf of Tunis, 30, 65

H

Hadjeb-el-Aioun, 126
Hansell, Brig. Gen. H. S., Jr., 91-92
Hartle, Maj. Gen. R. P., 90
Harwood, Adm. Sir Henry, 177
Hergla, 139
Hickey, Col. L. P., 82
Holland, 22
Horn, 12
Hurribomber, 24, 53, 118, 177
Hurricane, 14, 28, 187
HUSKY, 105, 143, 177

I

Iceland, 31, 90
Iraq, 90
Israel, Col. R. S., 87
Italian Air Force (IAF), 29, 62, 134-35, 153

J

Joint Chiefs of Staff, 2-3, 89
Jones, Maj. David, 31, 64
Ju-52, 10, 15, 34, 141-42
Ju-87 (Stuka), 19, 23, 29-30, 44-46, 124-25, 175, 186
Ju-88, 19, 26, 29, 34-35, 62, 67, 74, 77, 139, 141-42, 175
Juin, Gen., 13, 15, 115
JUPITER-GEMAST, 6

K

Kairouan, 31, 42, 66-68, 79, 110-13, 116, 152, 165, 176
Kalaa Djerda, 112

Kalaa Drira, 68
Kano, 154
Kasba, 23
Kasserine, 73, 116, 132, 142, 156, 175
Kasserine Pass, 72, 166, 169-75
Kebili, 42, 75, 113
King, Adm. Ernest, 155-56
Klocko, Lt. Col. R. P., 122
Koeltz, Gen., 15
Kuter, Brig. Gen. L. S., 92, 118, 125, 131, 165, 167-68, 185-86, 201 (n 12)

L

La Calle, 109
Lafayette Escadrille, 112-13, 119-20, 130, 158, 173
La Goulette, 56, 58, 150
La Hencha, 68, 160
La Senia, 8-9, 12, 68, 82
Lawson, Air Commodore G. M., 69, 98
Le Clerc, Gen., 144
Le Kef, 23, 28, 58, 76-77, 163
Le Kouif, 112, 167-68, 173
Liberator. See B-24.
Libya, 127, 144
Lightning. See P-38.
Lisbon, 22
Lloyd, Air Vice Marshal H. P., 181
London, 20
Luftwaffe. See German Air Force.

M

Me-200, 152-53
Mahares, 160
Maison Blanche, 11-15, 18-19, 21-22, 25, 28, 31, 35, 37, 39, 46, 48, 54, 59
Maison Carree, 98
Maknassy, 75, 78, 115-16, 123-24, 126, 128, 130, 164
Maktar, 117, 126
Malta, 53, 99, 135, 177, 179
Marauder. See B-26.
Mareth, 163, 176
Mareth Line, 42, 110, 114, 163

Mark-IX-D sight, 72
Marrakech, 9
Mascara, 48
Massicault, 39, 75
Mast, Gen. Charles, 11
Mateur, 16, 23, 28, 32, 35, 42, 75, 77, 161
Mateur-Sedjenane sector, 176
Mazagan, 8
Me-109, 18-19, 25, 29-32, 34-35, 38-39, 44, 54, 58, 62-63, 66-67, 70, 76-79, 123-24, 126-29, 139-42, 144-51, 160-62, 165
Me-109G, 76, 120
Me-109G1, 157
Me-109G2, 157-58
Me-110, 34, 139-41
Me-210, 140
Me-323, 142
Medenine, 42, 75, 127, 149
Mediouna, 9, 72
Mediterranean Air Command (MAC), 177-80, 188
Medjerda, 14, 48, 51, 85
Medjez-el-Bab, 16, 23, 27, 34, 39-40, 45
Meknes, 9, 48
Mers-el-Kebir, 9
Messerschmitt. See Me-109.
Mezzouna, 123
Middle East, 55, 91, 111, 177
  Commanders in Chief, 99
Middle East Air Command, 179
Mitchell. See B-25.
Mockler-Ferryman, Brig. D. C., 34
Mohamedia, 42
Momyer, Lt. Col. W. W., 72, 76
Montgomery, Gen., 42-43, 114, 185
Moroccan Composite Wing (MC), 82-83, 85-86
Morocco. See French; Spanish.
Mosquito, 137
Mostaganem, 24

N

9th Air Force, 42, 52, 90, 109, 178, 182.
IX Bomber Comd., 132
9th Div., 172
19th Engineer Regt., 170-71
XIX Corps, 115, 118, 177, 201 (n 12)
91st Fighter Sq., 113
92d Fighter Sq., 113
93d Bomb Gp., 55
94th Fighter Sq., 25, 34, 69, 71
97th Bomb Gp. (H), 10, 18-19, 21, 24-26, 30, 37, 39, 57-58, 60-61, 63, 128-29, 132, 144-52, 175-76
97th Bomb Sq. (L), 72
Naples, 53, 55, 134
Natal, 66
Nautilus, 63
Normandy, 187
North African Theater of Operations (NATOUSA), Hq of, 108
Northern Task Force, 85
North Quay (Bizerte), 30
North Quay (Sfax), 61
Northwest African Air Forces (NAAF), 56, 59, 170, 177, 179, 182, 184, 188
Northwest African Air Service Comd., 180-81
Northwest African Coastal Air Force, 180
Northwest African Photographic Reconnaissance Wing, 181
Northwest African Strategic Air Force (NASAF), 143, 171-72, 180
Northwest African Tactical Air Force (NATAF), 119, 170, 180, 184, 186-87
Northwest African Training Command, 180, 198 (n 73)
Nouvion, 22, 25, 59

O

154th Observation Squadron, 173, 187
168th Infantry, 165
Olds, Col. T. D., 22
Operations Div., ALGS, 155
Oran, 2-4, 6-11, 13, 17-18, 22, 25, 44, 47-48, 50, 54, 68, 70, 81-83, 86-87, 98, 109, 131, 134, 151, 154, 190 (n 9)
Oran Service Area Command (Prov), 83
Oudna, 27-28

Oued El Akarit, 144-45
Oued Hateb, 170, 172
Oued Zarga, 16
Oujda, 73, 82, 111
Ousseltia, 117-19, 122-23, 133, 126-27, 201 (n 12)

P

P-38, 12, 19-20, 22, 24-25, 28, 30, 32-33, 35, 37, 38-40, 45, 58-65, 67, 69-71, 74-78, 81, 112, 127-29, 136-50, 152-56, 158, 160-61, 175
P-38F, 26
P-39, 119-22, 124-25, 130, 154, 164-65, 169, 172, 174-75, 187
P-39D1, 121, 159
P-40, 8-9, 50, 66, 68, 74-79, 114, 119-20, 122-23, 125-26, 130, 159, 164, 166
P-40F, 72, 120, 126, 158
P-40N, 159
P-47, 156
P-400, 121, 159
Pacific, 90
Palermo, 55, 134, 151-52
Pantelleria, 138
Paratroop Task Force, 13
Park, Air Vice Marshal Sir Keith, 179
Patton, Gen., 8
Petrel, 63
Philippeville, 11, 48-49, 98, 109, 116
Phillips, Col. C. T., 55, 82
Pichon, 122, 126
Ploesti, 143
Polebrook, 18
Pont du Fahs, 27, 75, 115-17, 130
Portal, Sir Charles, 88-89, 158
Port Lyautey, 8, 9, 121
Porto Farina, 63
Portreath, 53-54
Portugal, 121
President, the. See Roosevelt.
Prime Minister. See Churchill.

R

Rabat, 9, 73
Rabat Sale, 9
RAF, 6, 19, 42, 44, 88, 92, 99, 100, 103, 118, 137, 153, 178, 180-81, 186
RAF Bomber Command, 53
RAF, Gibraltar, 178
RAF, ME, 42, 103, 145, 178
RAF, Malta, 178
RAF Malta Air Command, 179
Raff, Col. E. D., 13-14, 16, 21, 26, 69, 73
Rame, David, 43, 45
Ranger, U.S.S., 126, 155-56, 159
Ras El Ma, 48
Rask, Col. P. S., 85
Re-2001's, 151
Relizane, 59
Rhumel, 48-49
Ridenour, Col. C. H., 56, 60
Robaa, 117, 133, 201 (n 12)
Robb, Air Vice Marshal J. M., 103, 181
Roberts Field, 154
Robinett, Brig. Gen. P. L., 119, 171-72
Rommel, Field Marshal Erwin, 4, 43, 61, 66, 75, 85, 98, 109-10, 116, 145, 148, 163, 176, 185
Rommel's "Appreciation of Situation, 116, 163
Roosevelt, Lt. Col. Elliott, 181
Roosevelt, President, 2, 94, 97, 104
Rosanoff, Maj. Korstia, 120
Rouen, 18
ROUND-UP, 1-2, 88, 90, 92, 94, 97, 104
Royal Navy, 102, 134
Russia. See U.S.S.R.
Rutherford, Col. Alvord, 31

S

2d Air Defense Wing, 86-87, 180
2d Bn., 1st Armored Regt., 165
2d Bn., 5th Leicesters, 172
2d Bn., 503d Parachute Infantry, 13

II Corps, 85, 106, 109, 111, 115-16, 118, 123, 126, 128, 131, 163-64, 166, 170-71, 176-77, 180, 201 (n 12)
2d Fighter Sq., 24
2d Hampshires, 36
2d Service Area Comd. (Prov), 83
6th Armored Div., 117
7th Fighter Wing, 6, 60
  Headquarters, 60
17th Bomb Gp. (M), 66-68, 127, 129, 144, 146, 149, 151, 155, 160-61, 165, 168, 176
60th Troop Carrier Gp., 8, 12-13
62d Troop Carrier Gp., 9, 27, 190 (n 9)
64th Troop Carrier Gp., 12, 14
68th Observation Gp., 122, 125, 155, 167
78th Div., 23, 27, 69
78th Fighter Gp., 156
601st TD Battalion, 111
682 P.R. Sq., RAF, 181
701st TD Bn., 111
Safi, 9
St. Eval, 12
St. George Hotel, 98
Sardinia, 3, 15, 19, 20, 24, 29, 94-95, 105, 151
SATIN, 109-14, 116
SATIN Task Force, 110
Saunders, Air Vice Marshal A.P.M., 98
Saville, Brig. Gen. G. P., 84
Sbeitla, 51, 73, 112, 123, 166-69, 171, 176
Sbiba, 169, 171, 173
Schneider, Col. Max F., 155
Sebkra d'Oran, 12
Sedjenane, 176
Sened Station, 124-26, 130
Setif, 48, 53
Sfax, 16, 29, 31, 35, 42, 52-53, 56, 59-61, 63, 66, 68, 76-77, 110, 112, 114, 124, 127, 146-47, 149, 163
Siberia, 121
Sicilian Straits, 134-35, 142, 159, 177
Sicily, 3, 15, 20, 29, 65, 94-95, 105, 134, 152, 173, 187
Sidi Ahmed, 15, 18, 20, 29, 34, 39

Sidi Bou Zid, 73, 123, 164-65
Sidi Tabet, 35, 75-76
Siebel ferry, 141-42
Sierra Leone, 7
Sirius, H.M.S., 135
SLEDGEHAMMER, 1
Smith, Lt. Virgil, 75
Sommerfeld mat, 48, 51
Souk Ahras, 14, 109
Souk el Arba, 15, 23, 30, 43, 46, 48, 60, 76
Souk el Khemis, 48, 180
Sousse, 29, 52-53, 56, 59, 61, 64-65, 68-69, 78, 110, 116, 139, 146, 149, 152
Southwest Pacific, 136
Spaatz, Maj. Gen. Carl, 20, 51, 89-93, 97, 99-101, 106, 118, 131-32, 145-46, 156-57, 165, 170-71, 179-81, 184
Spain, 17, 22, 48, 81, 95, 98
Spanish Morocco, 3-4, 8, 17, 48, 80-81, 84, 95, 183
Spitfire, 14, 18, 19, 23, 28, 30, 39, 43, 48, 122, 127, 130, 156, 164-65, 168-69
Spitfire V, 26, 158
Spitfire IX, 158
Standard Oil Building, Algiers, 17
Strait of Gibraltar, 3-4, 51, 84, 95. See also Gibraltar.
Stuka. See Ju-87.

T

3d Air Defense Wing, 86-87
3d Paratroop Bn., 12
3d Photographic Gp., 181
3d Service Area Comd. (Prov), 83, 167
10th Panzer Div., 116
XII Air Force Service Comd., 83, 181
XII Air Support Comd., 6, 9, 17, 21, 47, 56, 60, 68, 72, 80, 82, 84-85, 87, 111, 113-14, 119, 123, 125, 127, 130, 132, 157-58, 164-67, 170-73, 175, 180, 183, 187, 197 (n 73)
XII Bomber Comd., 22, 26, 56, 59-60, 81, 127, 131, 133, 137, 143-44, 146-47, 149, 152, 155, 157, 165, 171, 195a (n 32)

XII Fighter Comd., 9, 17, 22, 32, 68-71, 77, 79, 82, 85-86, 157, 180, 183
12th Bomb Gp. (M), 162, 165, 172, 175
20th Air Force, 143, 182
21st Aviation Engineer Regt., 47
21st Panzer Div., 163
26th Armored Brigade, 171
26th Infantry, 171
26th Regimental Combat Team, 111, 119, 123
27th Light Bombardment Gp., 155
27th Fighter Sq., 62
31st Fighter Gp., 8-9, 18, 26, 126, 154, 156, 158, 165, 168, 172-74
33d Fighter Gp., 8-9, 50, 60, 66, 71-72, 112, 120, 124, 126, 153, 157, 173
58th Sq., 113
36th Brigade Gp., 11, 13, 28
242 Gp., MF, 69, 112, 118, 131, 170, 180, 186-87
301st Gp., 25-26, 57-61, 63, 128-29, 146-47, 149-52, 176
307th Sq., 172
308th Sq., 173
309th Sq., 172
310th Gp., 9, 35, 39, 49, 64, 66, 68, 129, 136-37, 139, 141-42, 149, 154, 160-61
319th Bomb Gp. (L), 21, 31-32, 34-35, 49, 64-67, 136, 138-40, 145, 154, 157, 160-61
320th Bomb Gp. (M), 155
321st Bomb Gp. (M), 155
323 Wing, 180
325 Wing, 180
325th Fighter Gp., 126, 155
326 Wing, 53
328 Wing, 180
340th Sq., 18
346th Sq., 168
350th Fighter Gp., 121-22, 168, 180
Tabarka, 13
Tafaraoui, 8-9, 17, 19-20, 22, 25, 30, 34, 46, 49, 54-55, 59
Tangier, 4
Taza, 8, 48
Tebessa, 13, 16, 21-22, 26-27, 50, 68, 77, 82, 85-86, 109-12, 116, 132, 162-63, 167-68, 170, 172-73

Tebourba, 23, 33, 36, 39, 42, 44
Tedder, Air Marshal Sir Arthur, 37, 53, 99-100, 106, 118, 132, 177-78, 184
Telergma, 48-49, 51, 82
Terrell, Lt. Col., F. R., 72
Thala, 162, 169-73, 177
Thelepte, 50-51, 66-67, 69, 72-75, 112-13, 120, 125-26, 130, 165, 167-69, 175
Timberlake, Brig. Gen. P. W., 178
TORCH, 1-2, 4-7, 18, 46-48, 53, 80, 88-91, 93-94, 96-97, 100-01, 103-04, 107, 121, 135, 153, 155, 183, 185
Trapani, 134, 151
Tripoli, 75, 114, 127, 147, 163, 185
Tripolitania, 42, 116
Tunis, 2-4, 10-11, 13-16, 20, 23, 27, 29, 32-37, 39, 42-43, 48, 51-52, 55-58, 61-63, 69-70, 73, 76, 85-86, 94, 100, 110, 136, 141, 146-47, 150, 161, 163
Turkey, 94

U

United Kingdom, 12, 53, 72, 89-90, 101, 107, 154-55. See also England.
U.S. Navy, 8
U.S.S.R., 1, 105, 121, 178

V

Vichyites, 120
Villacidro, 152
Von Arnim, 15, 33, 42, 110-11, 122, 176

W

Wade, Col. H. J., 121
Wadi Matratin, 109
Wadi Zemzem, 109
Wanamaker, Maj. W. L., 13-14
Wavell, 43
Wellington a/c, 53, 171, 180
Wellington III, 53
Welsh, Air Marshal Sir William, 4, 20-21, 30, 53, 69, 98-99, 111
Wertz, Maj. Jack, 121
Western Air Comd., 4

Western Algerian Composite Wing, 68, 82-83, 86
Western Desert, 135, 137
Western Desert Air Force, 106, 131, 180
Western Dorsal, 115, 163, 166, 168-69
Western Task Force, 4-5, 8, 17, 47, 90
Westover Field, 47
Wigglesworth, Air Vice Marshal H.E.P., 178
Williams, Col. Paul L., 10, 28, 82, 118, 124, 167, 180
Williams, Col. R. P., 93-95

Y, Z

Youks-les-Bains, 13, 21-22, 25-27, 30, 32, 34-35, 40, 44, 46, 50, 59, 62, 69-70, 72-73, 77, 99, 112, 167-68, 173-75
Ypres, 63
Zaghouan, 23, 42

www.ingramcontent.com/pod-product-compliance
Lightning Source LLC
Chambersburg PA
CBHW082117230426
43671CB00015B/2720